Culture Clash

The Death of a District Commissioner in the Loita Hills

Rupert Watson

ISBN# 978-9966-757-14-2

Published by Old Africa Books
A division of Kifaru Educational and Editorial Consultants Ltd
PO Box 2338, Naivasha, Kenya 20117

PREFACE

I can still see it now, the acre of Africa where I first heard the story of the spearing of a colonial officer by an angry young Maasai. I was fairly new to Kenya and in 1979 was staying a few days on a ranch not far from Nanyuki. After breakfast my host took me out to look at some cattle. These had been brought in early that morning and corralled in a large pen, fenced around with cedar posts and backed in the distance by the summit of Mount Kenya, still protruding above the gathering clouds.

The best of the cattle were to be sold, and as we leant on the top rail and he made casual jottings in a note book, the talk turned to the actual workings of the sale. They all looked like bullocks, but were they being sold for slaughter or would some be kept by the buyer for further fattening? Who indeed was to buy them and how would they leave the ranch, on foot or in wagons? I was not ashamed to admit my ignorance of the cattle trade in Kenya.

The beasts were as diversely coloured as cattle could be, and one particularly healthy bullock seemed determined to have its number included in the note book. It was generally black but with a white blaze on its face, and other white markings on its tummy and tail. 'That must look quite like the animal which the District Commissioner picked before he was killed,' said my host. 'Do you know the story?' No, I certainly didn't, and so out came his version.

I soon forgot much of what he told me, including both where it happened and the name of the officer who was killed. My imagination filled in a lot of the missing detail, moving the incident somewhere down east of Nairobi into the land of the Kamba, dressing the victim in shorts, long socks and a solar topee and standing him on a raised dais in the middle of the cattle pen. Still, enough lodged in the back of my mind so that when I rented a cottage on El Karama ranch in Laikipia a few years later, some relevant conversation helped me to the connection between the Grant family, owners of the ranch, and Hugh Grant which had emerged as the name of the dead DC.

Over the next many years, I heard occasional reference to the incident, and may even have steered talk in its direction. I learned that the killing took place in the Loita Hills and that the cattle selection was part of a compulsory purchase scheme. There was general agreement too that it occurred shortly after the end of the Second World War, but beyond this basic framework, the other details varied so much from one storyteller to another that I didn't absorb much more.

Several years later, I had a chance conversation with Bella Nicholson, granddaughter of Hugh Grant, in which she mentioned that her family had written his biography. Yes, it certainly did cover his death, she replied to my query, and yes, she could get me a copy when she was next up at El Karama, which she did.

Now armed with the exact date of his death, and having read so much about Hugh Grant in his biography, I had become even more intrigued by the whole story. So I asked Richard Ambani, a skilled researcher who knew his way around the National Archives as well as anyone, to see what he could find down there. Back came copies of the The East African Standard's reports on Grant's death as well as of one or two files with rather tangential references to it. The files gave fascinating insights into the *modus operandi* of the Kenyan administration in the 1940s but certainly not enough information to make Grant's death something to write about.

Then, almost as an afterthought, Ambani discovered the court file of the criminal trial of the man who had thrown the spear, Karambu ole Sendeu. In this was as much detail on the incident as I could ever hope to find anywhere. Further research was hugely helped by the surprising and welcome work of Syracuse University of New York in indexing a mass of pre-Independence material, and making it so readily available on the internet. This enabled me to give Ambani enough references for him to unearth the painstakingly prepared Handing Over Reports that DCs wrote up for their successors, as well as the Narok District's Annual Reports, which they were also required to submit. Diary excerpts, correspondence and internal memoranda all added a human dimension to the drier, more official accounts of events and proceedings.

While the documents from the archives were essentially colonial compositions, ironically what the court file really brought to the story was the Maasai perspective. The typed witness statements were all twice removed from what was spoken in the original Maa, having been translated first into Swahili, then into English, but here at least was the nearest I would ever get to hearing the voice of Karambu explaining why he threw the spear. Here too were the voices of the brothers who had arrested him and of Maasai elders telling the judge why their community was so tired of providing cattle for a compulsory purchase scheme, which had lasted for more than six years.

By the time I finished travelling around the Loita Hills, and talking with Loita Maasai, I was sure that this was a story worth telling and a record which needed setting straight. There is scope to interpret most historical events with some subjectivity and this one is no exception, which seemed another good reason to write about it. In the course of telling the story my own views began to move in a direction that actually surprised me, and while I have tried to keep them out of the narrative, they may colour some of the afterword. And if they do, so be it.

1

WHITE INTRUDERS

On 16 August 1946 the destinies of Karambu ole Sendeu, a young Maasai man from south-west Kenya, and Hugh Murray Grant, the District Commissioner for Narok, converged on the grassy plains of Morijo in the Loita Hills. Grant died that day from spear wounds, the weapon thrown with such force that it passed right through his torso and onto the dusty ground in front of him. For throwing that spear, Karambu had his neck broken by a hangman's noose in Nairobi Prison just over five months later.

From completely different ends of the human spectrum, Grant and Karambu could not have trodden more contrasting paths on their way to the cattle collecting pen, where their cultures collided with such tragic consequences. There, the two of them disagreed about the fate of a black, long-horned bullock, with a white tip to its tail, named Lemelelu, and so Karambu killed Grant.

Europeans and Maasai had confronted one another ever since the northerners began wending their various ways through East Africa, although, perhaps surprisingly, seldom with violent outcome. A reputation for hostility to outside intrusion had deterred coastal slaving parties from plying their miserable trade in most of the tribe's territory or from crossing through it with their cargoes. Later, the first white strangers muted valour with considerable discretion as they cautiously tested the Maasai temperament, at least until they had learned something of the ways of the indigenous people.

In 1883 the German explorer Gustav Fischer had beaten a strategic retreat from the shores of Lake Naivasha in the face of Maasai hostility, while attempting to become the first European to reach Lake Victoria through East Africa. A few months later, 26-year-old Joseph Thomson and his relatively small retinue of 113 porters fared better. Sponsored by the Royal Geographical Society and spurred by the possibility of Germans rather than the British being first to open up the interior of East Africa to the outside world, he showed what could be done with a blend of charm, humour and diplomacy. Thomson tempered all this with persuasive medicinal hocus pocus, which included removing his false teeth and contriving to froth at the mouth with the aid of fizzing Eno's liver salts. With such an unorthodox approach, the precocious young Scot was able to demonstrate that, notwithstanding the very real dangers, it was at least possible for foreigners to negotiate large tracts of Maasailand unharmed.

Thomson returned to the coast from Lake Victoria in May 1884, having successively avoided death from dysentery, malaria and the wounds inflicted on him by an injured buffalo. A year later, the Anglican missionary James Hannington arrived in Mombasa from England to assume his appointment as the first bishop of the huge diocese of Eastern Equatorial Africa. Spurred on by what he saw as his pivotal role in the expansion of the Anglican communion, he lost no time in heading off inland for Uganda with a small retinue of Christian porters. He too was able to negotiate Maasai territory unharmed - only to be murdered by the King of Buganda on the banks of the Nile. Generally though, with neither right nor might on their side, the early explorers, traders and missionaries did their best to avoid Maasailand. If they were not deterred by threats of attack, then clumsy attempts by the tribesmen to extort exorbitant gifts in exchange for safe passage often forced the intruders to find alternative routes to their destinations.

That there was actually so little aggressive resistance to the arrival of the Europeans - much less than the latter anticipated - also owed a lot to the sorry state of the Maasai nation in the last part of the nineteenth century. Intra-tribal fighting, particularly between the Purko and Laikipia Maasai in the north of their territory, had drastically weakened its social cohesion. Further strife followed on the death of the great leader, Mbatian, in 1890. His two sons, Lenana and Sendeu, fought bitterly over who should succeed their father, with Lenana's victory creating an enduring schism within the tribe, which continues to this day. Many of the tribe's young *moran* [warriors] lost their lives in these internecine conflicts, while outbreaks of cholera and smallpox respected neither gender nor age and took their toll on men and women, young and old. Drought and famine further weakened the tribe, killing both humans and animals, and even if livestock could find enough to eat and drink, their weakened condition made them particularly susceptible to rinderpest and bovine pleuropneumonia.

Having reluctantly relieved the Imperial British East Africa Company of its role in administering East Africa, the British Government declared it a protectorate on 15 June 1895. Not long afterwards, what became known as the Kedong Massacre looked set to give formal Anglo-Maasai relations a very shaky start. Yet perversely, despite its huge death toll, this shocking and little known affair seems to have served only to strengthen them. As with Hugh

Grant's death, it too involved the killing of a Briton by a Maasai spear, but although the common thread of cattle runs through both events, the circumstances surrounding them were vastly different.

On 25 November 1895 a huge caravan of over a thousand Kikuyu and coastal Swahili porters was on its way back from delivering supplies to the trading post of Eldama Ravine, then in Uganda and beyond what is now Nakuru. The caravan had reached the eastern edge of the Great Rift Valley, south of Lake Naivasha, and as it grew dark the Swahili headmen prompted the abduction of two local Maasai girls to supplement the evening's enjoyment. Exactly how events unfolded thereafter is unclear other than that the Maasai *moran* took this seizure of their womenfolk as a call to arms, and by the end of the following day over 600 porters lay dead, at a cost to the Maasai of the lives of less than 50 of their warriors.

Further down the Uganda road, Andrew 'Trader' Dick, in the company of three French hunters, was one of the first to hear of the massacre. Without pausing to ascertain the events leading up to it, he decided to take such law as there was into his own hands and mete out his version of punishment. This consisted of trying to kill as many Maasai as he could, not least in the hope of capturing large numbers of their livestock. With reluctant support from the Frenchmen, Dick rounded up 200 cattle and shot dead nearly 100 Maasai with his own rifle. This eventually jammed, allowing one of the surviving Maasai to catch up with him after a tortuous pursuit and kill him with a spear.

The official investigation which followed concluded that the Swahili headmen had provoked the Maasai, although it stopped short of condoning the violence of their reaction. It also found that if penalties were due, the Maasai had paid dearly enough with the death of so many of their *moran* following Dick's intervention, which it agreed was entirely unwarranted. Finally, the authorities ordered that the Maasai cattle captured by the trader be distributed among the families of the slain Kikuyu porters as some compensation for the death of their menfolk – and that was the end of it.

From their perspective, the Maasai had expected a much harsher reaction from the Europeans. Indeed their chief, Lenana, whom the British had supported in the succession struggles which followed his father's death, found cause for friendship rather than hostility in the almost Solomonic wisdom of the decisions. This set the tone for what was essentially a cooperative attitude, and one which dominated the rest of Lenana's dealings with the colonisers. Meanwhile, his followers remained in awe of the fire power which allowed one person to kill a hundred.

While convoys and caravans came and went through the land of the Maasai, usually with minimal impact on their lives, it was the decision to build a railway from Mombasa, on the Indian Ocean, to Lake Victoria, that really signalled the beginning of the end of their seclusion. The construction of the railway had effectively been part of British foreign policy since 1890 although its course through the passageways of power was a rough one indeed. The delays were largely occasioned by the British government's reluctance to assume responsibility for administering East Africa. Almost exactly a year after it accepted to do so, the Uganda Railway Bill was presented to parliament and in August 1896 funding for the railway was approved. Its proponents had been so frustrated at all the delays that they had actually begun construction several months earlier. A shortage of labour, as well as Mombasa's confusing island topography, made for a slow start to the laying of the track - meter wide to accommodate used rolling stock from India - and by the end of 1896 railhead had only moved 23 miles inland.

Initially, the British government had little interest in the land through which the rail would be laid, but rather in the perceived strategic advantages of linking Uganda with the nearest coast. Whichever European power controlled Uganda, so went the empire-building logic, would be able to extend its influence all the way down the Nile, through Sudan to Egypt and thus to the

Suez canal. And control of the canal meant control of all the shipping that passed through it. There could be positive social consequences too, which proponents of the railway were not slow to advertise. The mechanised transport for goods to and from the interior of the Dark Continent would soon replace the huge human caravans, still operating in conditions of near-slavery. However, for the time being at least, the promotion of any possible commercial gains from what The Times described as such a 'great and arduous undertaking', was held well in check.

The railway reached Mile 325 in May 1899 and so was founded Nairobi (*enkare nairobi* meant 'cold stream' in the Maasai language, Maa). It would be four years before the capital moved up there from Mombasa, but with the creeping expansion of urban sprawl the European presence gained an unassailable toehold on the edge of Maasai country. Thus did the balance of might began to tilt in favour of the new arrivals. So too, in the eyes of many of them, did the balance of right with the unilateral imposition of a centralized legal system over the whole of the protectorate.

The 'Lunatic Line' continued its unstoppable advance up the floor of the Rift Valley, bisecting the traditional Maasai grazing grounds around Naivasha and beyond. On 20 December 1901, engineer Preston's wife, Florence, drove the last spike into its last rail on the shores of Lake Victoria, 580 miles and five and a half years from its beginnings at Mombasa. The completion of the railway was cause for considerable national celebration back in England too. Nonetheless, the whole enterprise had cost around £5.5 million - more than double the budgeted amount. So while commercial considerations had originally been downplayed, the pressures to see the British government's investment in both railway and protectorate start to earn a return soon began to mount.

Large-scale farming, with the potential for export of its produce, seemed to offer the best chance of justifying the huge initial outlay on the railway. The Maasai never looked likely to adapt to the sedentary lifestyle of arable farmers, even in those parts of their territory suitable for cultivation. So a campaign was launched to attract white settlers by advertising the attractions of East Africa. These focused particularly on the temperate climate in the highlands between 4,000 and 8,000 feet and the potential for profitable ranching and agriculture, as well as on recreational opportunities. Not least to bring the whole of the Lunatic Line within the same colonial territory, the border between the British East Africa and Uganda Protectorates had, in 1902, with some sleight of the

London line drawer's hand, been moved west to encompass both ends of the railway. Now, with the protectorate's western boundary little different from that of today's Republic of Kenya, not only was the management of the railway made much easier, but there was also suddenly much more land available for settlement.

The response to the immigration campaign was enthusiastic and it was not long before South Africans of both English and Afrikaner descent - emotionally and financially drained by the aftermath of the Boer War - began to unload their lives off steamers in Mombasa harbour and onto the train bound for the treeless plains of Nairobi. Britons too joined the influx; no longer exploring or evangelizing, these were true immigrants, searching for their own piece of East African paradise. Reaching Nairobi, many of them then headed northwards, following the railway into the Rift Valley, where the land with the greatest agricultural promise was that of the Maasai.

Historically, Maasailand comprised one single, undivided swathe of country stretching from the Ewaso Nyiro river, north of Nanyuki, west to Lake Baringo, and down through the Rift Valley to the Tanganyikan border and beyond. The edges ebbed and flowed depending upon the fortunes of the tribe and its relations with neighbouring peoples, but thousands of Maasai woke every morning to distant views of Mount Kenya, which they revered as *Ol Doinyo Keri*, the 'black and white mountain'. Their cattle drank the waters of Lake Naivasha, raised the dust of the savannah up through Nakuru and grazed the rough grasslands of the Kinangop plateau. Theirs was, indeed, an often 'green and pleasant land'.

Many early settlers remarked on how sparsely populated much of the protectorate seemed to be. This was largely due to the pastoral nature of its indigenous peoples, whose seasonal migrations took them on great looping journeys through different parts of their country. In fact most pasture would be utilized for grazing at one time of year or another, and what might in some months have appeared vacant land to passing European eyes, was in fact just temporarily unoccupied. Nevertheless, the general perception that the Maasai had far more land than they needed was not easily dispelled, and it was certainly true that the combination of clan wars, drought and disease had dramatically reduced their numbers.

The Maasai 'used' or 'occupied' land and so long as they felt assured of its continued availability for the next generation, the question of ownership was irrelevant. The full right to its enjoyment was all that mattered and who enjoyed what land was largely a question of where they lived and what clan they belonged to. The land was never going to be sold, and the only way to lose it would be by defeat in battle with a neighbouring tribe. This communal form of tenure contrasted strongly with that to which the immigrants were accustomed. They came from countries where homes were built on privately owned plots, handed down from one generation to the next. 'An Englishman's home was his castle.' If the colonial administration was to respond effectively to the success of its campaign to attract new settlers, they had to be promised secure titles to their own tracts of land. These, in turn, had to be large enough to justify the huge risks most of the immigrants had taken in uprooting their families and moving to such unfamiliar territory.

In order to enable the grant of land titles, the administration needed first to get the land under its legal jurisdiction. So, with the stroke of a pen on the bottom of the East African (Lands) Order-in-Council of 1901 the Government gave itself control of the alienation of what was effectively all public land. Such sweeping powers were only marginally restricted the following year in the Crown Lands Ordinance, which disallowed the Commissioner for the East Africa Protectorate from alienating land '...in the actual occupation of natives'. Very little, if any, Maasai land fell within this exception. So the excision of large plots of land from the traditional Maasai grazing grounds, and the subsequent grant of legal titles by the newly established Land Department to white arrivals, began in earnest.

As the settler stream gathered momentum, it became clear to all but the most forceful proponents of European supremacy that, with the land available for Maasai use so rapidly contracting, it was time for some more formal recognition of the rights of the indigenous occupants. In 1902 the office of Commissioner for the East Africa Protectorate was occupied by Sir Charles Eliot and unfortunately for the Maasai, he was not the one to legalise any such recognition. A phenomenal linguist with wide-ranging interests, which included Buddhism and marine biology, Eliot was inclined to support the immigrants where their interests opposed those of the pastoralists. Finding himself unable to fulfill promises to grant certain would-be settlers large tracts of land in the middle of prime Maasai grazing areas, he began an acrimonious correspondence with the Foreign Secretary, Lord Lansdowne. This culminated in Eliot's resignation in 1904 and a year later in his book *The East Africa Protectorate*, he would write that 'Natives must be protected from unjust aggression and be secured sufficient land for their wants; but with that proviso I think we should recognize European interests are paramount'.

Hugh Cholmondeley, Lord Delamere, had trekked into the protectorate from British Somaliland in 1897 and ever since had been in the forefront of encouraging white settlement. Unsurprisingly, his views were largely similar to those of Eliot, but he blended these with much greater foresight and a deeper understanding of his adopted homeland. Unable to omit his inevitable criticism of its administration by the faraway British Government, he summed up with extraordinary perception – and no little self interest – how...

> The Maasai occupy or partially occupy a very large tract of country, and in parts of it the Foreign Office have allowed settlers to take up land without any arrangements apparently being come to with the Maasai... Now it does not appear to me possible that, although these people are perfectly friendly, unprotected settlers could live side by side with them without sooner or later some serious misunderstanding occurring, without possibly any fault on either side... It does not appear to me fair, either on the settler or on the Maasai that the Foreign Office, simply because it does not take the trouble to have any policy in the matter, should expose them both to such misfortunes.

It would seem much fairer to tell the Maasai once and for all that we have come to stay and to give then a certain tract of country in which they would not be disturbed. This system would have many other advantages, as the chief would have more power. At present we pretend to govern the Maasai and yet we try to make Lenana responsible...

This seems to me the only way to deal with pastoral natives possessing large flocks and herds, who live in a country likely to be settled by white men. The reservation would have to be carefully chosen, not by someone fresh out from home looking at the country just after the rains. In the case of the Maasai, who from pride do not eat game and therefore do not kill it, a native reservation might very well be combined with a reserve for the game which might be in it.

Eliot's place was taken by Sir Donald Stewart who arrived on 1 August 1904 with instructions from the Foreign Office that 'The primary duty of Great Britain in East Africa is the welfare of the native races'. Whether as a result of, or in spite of, Delamere's views, Stewart found that the Administration had already pushed on with plans for the creation of specific areas for Maasai occupation. In return for the inhabitants of the Rift Valley and Kinangop plateau agreeing to move out of their ancestral territories, Maasailand was to be formally demarcated into two areas, specifically designated the Northern and Southern Maasai Reserves and linked by a connecting corridor. These were promised to their occupants for 'so long as the Maasai as a race shall exist' and Stewart hardly had time to get his feet under the desk before he was signing a formal agreement with the Maasai, which began...

> We, the Undersigned, being the Lybons and Chiefs (representatives) of the existing clans and sections of the Maasai tribes in East Africa Protectorate, having, this 9th day of August, 1904, met Sir Donald Stewart, His Majesty's Commissioner for the East Africa Protectorate and discussed fully the question of a land settlement scheme for the Maasai, have, of our own free will, decided that it is for our best interests to remove our people, flocks, and herds into definite reservations away from the railway line, and away from any land that may be thrown open to European settlement.

The seeming willingness of the Maasai to relinquish all rights to so much of their original territory is often attributed to the British Government's taking unfair advantage of the tribe's illiterate leaders. Certainly all the Maasai executed the treaty with marks, not signatures, but if this was really the case, then it brands Lenana and his chiefs as an easily manipulated group of primitives prepared to surrender the best interests of their people for fear of alienating better armed invaders. And this they certainly were not. Lenana was shrewd and intelligent but tended to lead more with his head than his heart. Taking a pragmatic approach, he knew his tribe was so weakened that its original territory was actually far more than it could ever defend in the foreseeable future - with or without the arrival of the immigrants. Nor would he have been blind to the fact that, just as Delamere had pointed out, his own position would be much strengthened by the creation of an exclusive, legally recognized, homeland where Maasai law and custom generally prevailed.

Shifting so many Maasai northwards freed up further large areas of land for allocation. This was as well for there seemed to be no stemming the enthusiasm of would-be settlers. East Africa's profile beyond its borders had been boosted by a visit from Joseph Chamberlain, as Secretary of State for the Colonies, in 1902, during which he rode a long stretch of the railway. Five years later the fledgling protectorate would receive Winston Churchill (as Undersecretary of State for the Colonies, the British Colonial Office having taken over responsibility for the protectorate in April 1905 from the Foreign Office). Then in 1909, former United States President Theodore Roosevelt would come hunting and 'collecting', accompanied by his son Kermit and a retinue of some 250 porters and guides. Many other celebrities were particularly attracted by the chance to shoot big game and the Administration was in danger of becoming a victim of its own success in recruiting immigrants unless still more land could be found to satisfy the demand.

Inevitably, it was the native pastoralists who were again seen as being most easily able to appease the settlers' land hunger. Notwithstanding the continued existence of 'the Maasai as a race', just seven years after the 1904 treaty the colonial authorities were attempting to renegotiate it. The incentive for the Maasai was the creation of one single reserve, which would certainly have strengthened Lenana's control over Maasailand as a whole had he not died just before the April 1911 Maasai Agreement was executed. This was marked by his son Segi, who took over as paramount chief, and by a rather disparate collection of other Maasai leaders and elders who all impressed their thumbprints on a treaty by which they undertook '...to vacate at such time as the Governor may direct the Northern Maasai Reserve which we have hitherto inhabited and occupied and to remove by such routes as the Governor may notify to us our people, herds and flocks to such area on the south side of the Uganda Railway as the Governor may locate to us'.

Unbeknownst to the Colonial Office, the then Governor, Sir Percy Girouard, an erstwhile railway engineer of French Canadian extraction, had actually begun promising tracts of Laikipia, in the heart of the Northern Reserve, to European settlers even before 1911. Girouard had spent time running the railways in South Africa where he had acquired a wife as well as some fairly Eurocentric views. So once given at least some sort of authority by the Agreement, however questionable, he was not slow to set in train the Maasai exodus. In June that year, perhaps 10,000 humans, some 200,000 cattle and nearer two than one million sheep, set off from Laikipia along their own 'trail of tears' en route for the newly promised land of a much enlarged Southern Maasai Reserve. Two months later, as different columns of migrants converged on the uplands of the Mau escarpment, rain, cold and lack of grazing halted any progress, forcing families and animals down into the lower levels of the Rift Valley or even to retrace their steps back from whence they came.

Girouard's pre-emptive actions had forced the Administration into an uneasy corner, and the whole affair reverberated very uneasily down the corridors of the

Colonial Office in London. The following year Girouard resigned in some disgrace – although not before securing a lucrative managerial post in the private sector – and the Maasai began an unsuccessful court action to have the 1911 Agreement annulled. This was brought principally on the grounds that the chiefs who executed it had no basis to do so and their views did not properly represent those of most of their fellows. While the case continued, so did the movement of the Maasai and by the end of March 1913 the greater part of the northern Maasai had finally trekked southwards to face the uncertainties of a new homeland.

The official report of this massive rearrangement of Maasai territory was set out in the East Africa Protectorate's Blue Book. These were the yearly reports of each British territory, giving details of finances, legislation, public works, personnel, populations and much more. That for 1911 described how 'an area of 4,500 square miles on Laikipia, of which not more than 1,200 was well watered, was to be exchanged for 6,500 square miles in the south, of which 1,500 was described as some of the best stock country in British East Africa, and through the remaining 5,000 square miles of which flowed two perennial rivers'.

This rose-tinted write-up is unlikely to have reflected the real views of anyone in the Administration. The

Southern Maasai Reserve had been much extended to accommodate the huge influx of families and livestock from the north. Indeed, one of the principal incentives used to persuade the northern Maasai to move south was that their doing so would unite most of the East Africa Protectorate's branch of the tribe in one single contiguous territory. Yet while this extension may have more than compensated for the abandoned grazing lands in area, many Maasai perceived its quality to be sorely inferior to the land they had left behind.

Rainfall in the larger, newly created reserve was generally much less than in Laikipia, and the Maasai cattle had to share their grazing with huge herds of plains game. Unfamiliar ticks and tsetse flies, as well as bacteria-borne diseases, all took their toll on the domestic animals, and in the lower lying areas humans began to contract malaria. Besides the difficulties in adapting to this new environment, intra-tribal conflicts between the displaced Purko and the long-established Loita Maasai were almost inevitable. The 'hosts' found themselves being squeezed out of the Loita Plains and up into the hills, and as too many animals began to compete for too little grazing the land inevitably began to degrade. Nor would it be long before government-imposed quarantine regulations served to further increase tensions by restricting cattle movements within the single reserve.

This wholesale uprooting of the Purko Maasai from Laikipia left a long-lasting bitterness in the hearts of almost every member of the tribe. It soured the Administration's relations with the Maasai for years afterwards and still stains the history of the colonial management of Kenya. Many of the survivors of that translocation were still alive when Hugh Grant took over as District Commissioner in 1946, and continued to regard cooperation with the architects of that traumatic displacement as little short of treasonable. One of Grant's successors as DC Narok, R. A. Wilkinson, wrote with particular candour in his 1951 Handing Over Report to J. Pinney that...

> The third reason [why the Maasai are so reluctant to change their ways], and perhaps the most important, is a rooted distrust of the government by the Maasai. This arises chiefly from their treatment in land matters and in particular the move of the Purko from Laikipia, which many of the chiefs remember. If you travel outside the district with Maasai you will find few places which they do not regard as Maasai land. Chief ole Sangale has shown me where he lived in his father's *manyatta* [fenced enclosure] as a boy; it is now the Nyeri polo ground. Rightly or wrongly all

this rankles and whenever an unpopular innovation is proposed in a *baraza* [meeting] you will hear angry references to Laikipia...

In February the following year the Duke of Edinburgh would play polo at Nyeri polo ground, two days before his wife, Princess Elizabeth, succeeded to the throne of the United Kingdom of Great Britain and Northern Ireland. Eight months later, Kikuyu Mau Mau insurgents reduced the club buildings to ashes and in the same month the Kenya government declared a State of Emergency, which lasted right up to 12th January 1960.

2

KARAMBU OLE SENDEU

The Loita Hills are surely one of the most spectacularly beautiful parts of East Africa. They rise up from the Nguruman Escarpment on the west side of the Great Rift Valley, ridge after ridge rolling away towards Kenya's Maasai Mara reserve and down southward into Tanzania. A patchwork of grassland and forest cover the slopes, boggy swamps stretch along the valleys, before the hills give way to huge sweeping plains. These are dotted with herds of both wild and domestic animals, the two often distinguished in the distance only by the scarlet *shukas* [cloaks] of the herdsmen watching over the livestock.

On the death of Mbatian in 1890, with the majority of the Maasai supporting his son Lenana in the succession struggles, his other son, Sendeu was left to take refuge amongst those few who had sided with him - principally the Sirin and Loita Maasai. Having led his extended family up into the Loita Hills,

Siria? DOWN?

he settled down among his hosts, and in the process established the nucleus of the Engedongi section of the Loita Maasai.

Karambu was one of Sendeu's children (*ole Sendeu* meaning 'child of Sendeu'), born in the Engedongi heartland of Kisokon, at the upper end of a wide, shallow valley and an easy three hours walk from the veterinary centre of Morijo. The Engedongi section remained a class apart from the rest of the Loita Maasai, the men distinguished by the leather thong they wore around their ankles, and their cattle marked with distinctive brands as well as the mark of the individual owner. Most significantly, the section provided *laibons* for the Loita Maasai as a whole. *Laibons* were the ritual and spiritual leaders whose authority was based on mystical gifts, which purportedly endowed them with supernatural powers. Sendeu had been absorbed into the Loita clan as its chief *laibon*, the position his father Mbatian had occupied for the tribe as a whole.

While the *laibons* gradually began to take on political roles, their prime responsibility remained to act as a channel between society and the higher powers that guided it. Purporting to divine the intentions of the supernatural through soothsaying and ceremony, they also played the part of traditional healers, nurturing reputations through a more profound knowl-

edge of plants and their properties than lesser mortals could ever acquire. The *laibons* used a variety of herbs, stones, shells and other paraphernalia in their divinations. All these were usually carried in a cow horn or a calabash gourd, picked from the creeping vine known to science as *Lagenaria siceraria* and to the Maasai as *engedong* from which the Engedongi section took its name. Draceana/Cordyline.
Kedong River.

Of the *laibons*' many functions, ensuring peace among the various sections of the tribe and protecting it from outside aggression were uppermost. One way to divert the focus of warrior attentions away from the livestock of their own Maasai neighbours was to sanction, even encourage, raiding expeditions into the bordering territories of other tribes – for the Loita Maasai usually down into Tanganyika to the lands of the Kuria and Sukuma. Prior to such forays, the spokesmen for those warriors involved in the raiding plans would visit the *laibon* to gain his approval of their intentions as well as protection from the injuries that would otherwise inevitably ensue. Such a role was scarcely calculated to endear the *laibons* to the British colonial authorities, nor was the suspicion that *laibons* were usually behind the not infrequent expressions of Maasai discontent. These often manifested themselves in outbreaks of civil disobedience, and as chief *laibon* Sendeu was regarded as a prime source of trouble.

By the time Hugh Grant took over from E. H. Windley as District Commissioner of Narok in March 1946, Sendeu had been dead for some ten years. When one administrative officer passed the baton to another, the incomer would be guided by a meticulously prepared Handing Over Report compiled by his predecessor. In Windley's report, he advised that 'the Maasai are fairly free from the political activity evinced by the Kikuyu...' and then went on to give a somewhat ambivalent overview of the history and function of the *laibons*, which also put Karambu's extended family in its wider context:

> The Sirin and Loita deal with the Sendeu branch who live in the Loita and whose head is Simil who is more respectable and amenable than most *laibons*. On the whole they perform many benign functions in directing and blessing tribal functions. It is generally the quacks who deal in stock raiders' charms. As you may know, Mbatian was the greatest Maasai *laibon* who first made contact with the Europeans and decided to sway the Maasai into friendship with them. He had a brother called Nelion, whose descendants live in the Loita and sometimes come into the picture. Mbatian's two sons, Lenana and Sendeu, split like

Jacob and Esau and their followers fought for years. Now their descendants still distrust each other and the Sendeu live in the Loita (Narok District) and the Lenanas in Kajiado District. They [*laibons*] are an integral part of the tribal life and not an entirely malign influence...

***

Karambu ole Sendeu lived for about 25 years - half as long as Hugh Grant - and the most reliable record of his birth would have been his mother's memory. The medical officer, W. E. Lawes, who examined Karambu in custody, aged him around 30, adding that the Maasai had 'no real knowledge of his age'. Those of his fellows questioned at his murder trial put him nearer 20.

The only written details of Karambu's existence are contained in the transcripts of the court proceedings of his trial. In these are recorded only sketchy references to his character and background. Nonetheless, the strictness of the Maasai social structure was such that the stages of childhood, boyhood, circumcision, *moran*, junior elder and senior elder were as immutable as the sequence of the seasons. From these, it is not hard to paint a picture of Karambu's life, and the social environment in which he lived it. There was very little scope to deviate from these pre-ordained steps to maturity. Almost the only element of choice in growing up a Maasai boy derived from the provision by the Administration of basic education facilities for young male children; and in practice few fathers were prepared to lose the labour of a young son long enough to see him through school.

Karambu's father was either absent or dead for most of his formative years, having been banished by the Administration from the Loita area some time after the end of the First World War. The justification for this seemingly draconian decision was based on the suspicion of his being one of the principal instigators of more active Maasai resistance to colonial domination. Not long after his return from exile he died from an epileptic fit, when Karambu, according to his elder brother Ranan in evidence, 'was still a small child and herding calves'.

Without a father's influence on his upbringing Karambu was perhaps spared frequent doses of rabid anti-British sentiment. The environment in which the boy was raised is likely to have been one in which British colonial dominance was, at best, reluctantly tolerated as a necessary evil. The displaced Purko may have lived apart from the indigenous Loita Maasai, both socially and geographically, but the Purko's move from Laikipia and the contraction of greater Maasailand into the single reserve, had gradually evolved into a collective affront to every member of the tribe. This would not have been lost on the young Karambu.

Most of Karambu's childhood play had a purpose. Mock fighting was practice for the real thing, as was shooting blunted arrows with bows whose strings he had been taught to twist from the fibres of wild sisal leaves. He would need to learn how to make sticks and clubs, and as one of a group of variously aged children he might have hunted small animals with packs of dogs - usually the ones to benefit from anything they caught. Older children might have taught him to distinguish nutritious fruits from poisonous ones and as he matured he would have absorbed more detailed knowledge of the traditional uses of different plants. He would also need to be able to make a fire and to know how, in times of drought, to pack up and move on in search of greener pastures.

Boys usually had very little to do with their mothers. While Karambu may have lacked guidance from his biological father, there would have been no shortage of other elders prepared to counsel him through his early life, and up to that fundamental rite of passage for all young Maasai - circumcision (*emurata*). As a growing child his most important contribution to the community was to show himself capable of watching over large herds of grazing livestock. Starting with newly weaned kids and lambs, he moved on to young calves and finally full sized cattle, from all of which he was expected to deter any marauding predators. His temperament and character were under continual scrutiny, elders watching to see that he was not intimidated by his age mates or others from his own clan. Nor could his physique be ignored; once circumcised and a fully-fledged warrior, he needed to carry heavy weapons and fight battles for his people.

Enduring pain bravely was one of the essential attributes of a male Maasai, and Karambu is often likely to have felt he was being tested. As a child he most likely had his two lower middle teeth removed, quite possibly by his mother while he sat in the centre of a circle of his peers, each already keen to see if he showed any signs of pain. Self-inflicting wounds on his own skin was good practice for the trauma of real injury and Karambu and his friends would have scarred their thighs with burning cloth or coals. Other scarifications could be effected by breaking thorns off the branches of acacia trees, pushing these through the skin, then adding irritants which left a puckered surface that remained with them for the rest of their lives. His mother probably pierced his upper ears with hot metal spikes at the same time as irons were being heated for branding the cattle. Later a chunk of his earlobe would have been cut out and the hole filled with a clay plug. Then came the real test when it was time for his *emurata*, probably soon after the onset of puberty.

There are intense pressures on young boys about to be circumcised. Eyes should be kept open all the time. The slightest response to the knife cut, even a silent squeeze shut of the eyes, let alone any verbal exclamation, can bring lifelong shame not only upon the circumcised, but also his whole extended family. After a sleepless night, Karambu most likely spent the dawn hours before his own time came outside his village, beside the nearest stream or water hole. There, as the grey sky lightened he numbed his extremities with the chill of the morning before returning to the ceremonial stage of his initiation, on the right-hand side of the entrance to his late father's *manyatta*. As friends urged him be strong with words of encouragement, or even taunted him with threats of the dire consequences of failure, he was cleansed of all his boyhood misdeeds with more water poured over him from a ceremonial ceramic pot. Finally he yielded to the supportive arms of a family elder and awaited the ultimate test of his fortitude.

So eager are young men to join the elite group of *moran*, that their enthusiasm may go some way towards dulling the instinctive response to wince under the circumcision knife. Very few of them do, and surely Karambu did not. Thus, perhaps aged around 14, he left his childhood behind on the cowskin where he lay while his foreskin was agonizingly removed. The rite of passage had now forced him to exchange the secure and comfortable family environment for the high testosterone company of other newly circumcised young men.

All in their physical prime of life, the *moran* spent time together in the same *manyatta*, cementing lifelong relationships through the bonds of shared food and friendship, as well as common danger and excitement. Their independent status as warriors symbolized the autonomy of the standing army of their tribe and its responsibilities for security of life and livestock. With the cut of a knife Karambu's role in society had changed from that of protected to protector.

While recovering from his injury, Karambu joined other initiates, each wrapping black cloaks around their bodies and daubing white clay all over their faces. He may already have fashioned a headdress made up of the skins of brightly coloured birds, knocked out of the branches with small clubs especially designed for accurate throwing. Remaining in this limbo stage until fully healed, his head would have then been shaved again and his black cloth shed, allowing him to emerge as a fully fledged Maasai warrior. Hav-

ing cast off the shackles of childhood, he
swerable to no-one - and free to have sex
but only uncircumcised girls.

Male Maasai society is divided chronologic   y into
age groups, each beginning as another ends. The time
of a boy's circumcision determines the age group he
joins. Each group unites its members in a fraternity of
warriors enduring for up to seven years, at the end of
which its members graduate to the following stage of
life and the next age group takes over. Within a group
are two sections, the right and left hands, the right
entering warriorhood as the left hand of the previous
age group ends; these then make way for the left of
their own group, who carry the warriors' mantle until
becoming junior elders and the whole cycle starts again.

As Karambu grew to fill the role of warrior
bestowed upon him by circumcision, so his hair
lengthened, the long, ochred locks signifying his status
of *moran* as certainly as any uniform. Banding together
with the other *moran* of his age group, and equipped
with spear, club and sword, he and his friends roamed
Maasailand in small groups, hunting lions, and perhaps
buffalo, whose hides they fashioned into shields. With
the consent of the *laibons* - usually easily gained - they
raided their Tanganyikan neighbours for cattle, all the
while providing security for the Engedongi clan.

ᴄattle raids were the apogee of *moran* life, giving each the opportunity to prove himself before his peers and the rest of the community. Setting out to capture livestock from a neighbouring tribe, the *moran* would travel at night, resting up by day, if possible in the thicker cover growing along a river bank. On their way they noted the best and fastest return route for driving back the cattle they hoped to steal. Nearing their objective, the main party stayed hidden while scouts went up to spy out where the cattle were corralled. Then, when night and quiet had descended on the village, they all crept up closer before splitting into smaller groups. Some were detailed to open the gate of the cattle *boma* and drive out the animals, while others stayed behind to deter pursuit. As the stolen herd moved homewards, a few cattle would inevitably fail to keep up with the pace and have to be abandoned; others would stray away from the main group and take more time to recover than the raiders could afford. If they eventually reached home still with plenty of animals, one would be killed for the celebrations, which lasted long into the night – especially if they were not muted with mourning for the death of *moran* killed in the raid.

Lion hunts also gave the young men the chance to show their bravery. He who threw the first spear into the lion was awarded its mane, irrespective of the injury the weapon caused the animal; the thrower of the second got the tail and the third the claws. If Karambu had earned any of these honours, his brothers are likely to have mentioned this in their evidence, or someone else would have remarked on his entitlement to wear lion body parts, and if they did, this is not recorded. Karambu was remembered by his cousin Merepari ole Tipoti as being 'liable to quick temper' but not 'a man who loses his temper for no good cause all the time'; otherwise, little was said at his trial about his character or his time as a *moran*.

So the wild carefree days continued for up to seven years until the elders deemed the warrior age-set to have completed its service. By then its members were responsible enough to have earned the status of senior warrior, or junior elder, and so to be replaced by a new set of *moran*, anxiously pressing at the heels of the retiring warriors to succeed them. The dates of successive age groups are as well known to Maasai as those of monarchs or presidents are to students of European or American history. Karambu was of the right hand of the *Ilnyangusi* age group, which graduated to junior elders in 1945 just as the left hand replaced them. So by the middle of 1946 he was, in name at least, no longer a *moran*. Yet the traits of warriorhood are not shed easily, and while the days of wandering Maasailand with a group of fellow adventurers were over, he had yet to marry, and would have taken any opportunity that presented itself to rekindle some of his old warrior ways.

The graduation of Karambu's age group to junior elders in 1945 took place in a communal ceremony known as *eunoto,* shortly followed by each participant retiring to drink the first milk to have passed his lips since circumcision. No weapons were carried during the celebrations and it was crucial to this transition for every *moran* to have his hair shaved, usually by his mother. Once done, the retiring *moran* then comprised a reserve army, and with the heady days of cattle raiding over, they were allowed to go home, marry and raise families. This time in auxiliary service was expected to last until, moving through a sequence of further ceremonies culminating in *olng'esher,* the junior elders were ushered into true elderhood.

Karambu was never to become a full elder but his status as a newly promoted junior elder was endorsed by several witnesses at his trial. Lawes, the medical officer, after examining Karambu, declared himself of the opinion that he had 'recently graduated from the *moran* stage', while Merepari ole Topoti, with a cousin's first-hand perspective, was clear at the trial that 'the Accused is the same circumcision age as myself. I have passed out of the *moran* stage and am a *mzee* [old person].' Kitona ole Sakaya, a Maasai employee at the

Native Civil Hospital in Narok, also suggested that 'the Accused is between 24 and 30. The Accused is not a *moran* now, as I see he has no pigtail.'

Of course, if Karambu had long hair when he was arrested, he would have been barbered in gaol, but the most likely shaver of his head was his mother, as he left behind him his ochred dreadlocks and the glory days of the warrior. She never featured in any of the reports of the trial, but when the answers were typed onto Prison Form No. 42, late in 1946, it is shown she was then alive. Headed 'Medical Report upon Prisoner Remanded on a Capital Charge', if these answers are accurate they also show Karambu was neither married nor had any children when he came to be hanged.

3

HUGH MURRAY GRANT

Hugh Grant was a warrior too, brought up in a society only a little less structured than the one through which Karambu had advanced. His father came from a long line of Scottish highland landowners, but with primogeniture so firmly enshrined in the British upper classes, younger children often had to follow their own stars away from the ancestral birthplace. As the fifth and last child of the Laird of Glenmoriston, near Inverness, Grant's father, Frank, had followed his star to Manchester where, with commercial enterprise uncharacteristic of his upbringing, he carved out a life for himself in the cotton industry – and found a wife. The fortune he acquired there would later enable him to buy part of the Glenmoriston family estate from his elder brother, Murray, who had inherited the lairdship; and by so doing Frank was able to restore the connection of his branch of the family with the highlands of Scotland that was so critical to its identity.

Born on 22 January 1897, Hugh was the second of the ten surviving children his parents produced, and while there was no preordained road for him to follow, as there was for Karambu, some form of public service was a natural career choice for many younger sons old enough to choose. In 1915, however, as Europe set itself on an irrevocable course of self-destruction, there was not much choosing to be done, and after undertaking a war-shortened training course for officers at the Royal Military Academy Sandhurst, the only decision he had to make was which regiment to join. And with the Grant family's long-standing connections to the Queen's Own Cameron Highlanders this was quickly put beyond choice as well.

The hell of the Western Front moulded 18-year-old characters in unimaginable ways. Beyond any doubt Grant was very brave, and this must have enabled him to bear some of the war's horrors better than others did. He made as light as he could of the misery of trench life in his letters home, probably aware both of the need to appease the mail censors and to spare his parents any further anguish than his absence already caused them. His boarding-school years at Eton would have helped him adapt to army discipline and he clearly seems to have been at ease in the all male military environment.

Having spent so much time on the sporting stage of a highland estate, Grant was well used to handling knives and guns. Nonetheless, it is no surprise that he addressed his pencilled letter of 21 August 1918 to his father rather than his mother:

> By the way, it might interest Wyn to know that I slew a Boshe with that little knife he gave me. Three of us went out and did in a post. Six killed and one shot in the tummy so he should die too. We all got away. The sentry was dozing and went west first of all with the knife in the back of the neck.

Is this just British understatement, or was it really in Grant's nature to recount a grisly incident like this with such casual insouciance – and in the true language of the overgrown schoolboy? But then, like so many of his fellows sent out to the trenches, that is exactly what he was – young in years, but old far beyond those years in what he had experienced and endured.

By August 1918, only three months away from the Armistice, he had been awarded two Military Crosses. His first came on 19 July 1918, the citation reading...

> Lt (Temporary Captain) Hugh Murray Grant, MC, Cameron Highlanders, attached 5th Battalion.

> For conspicuous gallantry in command of a support company in the attack. When the leading company was held up by machine-gun fire, he led up a portion of his own company and carried the line forward. Later, as a machine-gun crew left a dugout he dashed forward and shot the officer and made the crew prisoners. Throughout the day he set a magnificent example of courage.

Just two weeks later, on 3 August, he received the bar to his MC.

> This officer, with two other ranks, attacked an enemy machine gun about 400 yards in front of our position in broad daylight, capturing the gun and accounting for all the garrison of the post. He returned to our lines having obtained a valuable identification. His gallantry and initiative were worthy of high praise.

With the war over and most of his friends and colleagues demobilized from the army and feeling their tentative ways into civilian life, Hugh was off to Russia. The North Russian Relief Force was raised from former servicemen, who volunteered to join an expedition to Archangel. This was intended both to strike a decisive blow at the Bolsheviks on the Dvina River and to help provide an escape route for British soldiers who had been supporting the White Russian opposition throughout the winter. It is unlikely to have been lost on Grant that there would be excellent chances of good fishing up there, and as soon as the force arrived in Archangel in early June 1919, it immediately began training for an offensive. This was launched in early August with spectacular success and minimal casualties, and by early October both the force and the troops it had relieved were on their way home.

Returned to Britain, the closest Grant could get to active service was helping keep an uneasy peace in Ireland. There he found himself deeply frustrated by a status quo which strongly discouraged any retaliation against Sinn Fein Republicans, notwithstanding their continual sniping away at him and his companions. Despite forays into field sports - 'we shot a lot of rabbits and I got a wild swan with the big gun' - this brand of post-war army life held little excitement for one who had joined his regiment as an officer in France at the age of 18, knifed a German sentry in the neck and been awarded two MCs before the war was over. Travel might to some extent compensate and Grant was overjoyed when his application for secondment to the King's African Rifles was accepted. By the end of 1921 he was on his way to Kenya.

His tours of KAR duty took him first up to Lodwar, close to the western shores of Lake Rudolf. This was to be the first of many postings, whether as army officer or colonial administrator, to the borders of what had become known as the Northern Frontier District. There he remained for over a year, filling the role of soldier, administrator and policeman in this hot, dry yet captivating wilderness. For much of his posting his mercurial superior, Captain the Baron Eric von Otter, was away and Grant had few resources to fall back upon other than his own. This seems to have helped him quickly develop confidence in his ability to act independently and it was not long before he was able to write in one of his letters how 'one almost gets to resent any interference from the outside world'.

Like von Otter he too travelled as much as he could around the district, not least to try and control cattle rustling, ivory poaching and the many other illegal activities of generally uncontrollable people. He often camped on the shores of the lake from where he 'popped crocs and got a good bull hippo'. Grant was a wonderful correspondent and it is clear from his frequent and most endearing letters home, that the pursuit of game continued to feature large in his outpost life. 'The gun you sent is a beauty. I got three geese with it the other night…' Like many of his kind, he was also a great observer of the natural world and often remarked in his letters on the variety of bird species around wherever he happened to be, naming as many as he could.

One of the legacies left to Grant by the First World War was a large piece of shrapnel in one of his legs, which became infected while he was up in Lodwar, forcing evacuation to Nairobi. There he was given the job of running the battalion's depot, organizing polo weekends and other social activities.

Although clearly a very companionable character, there was a more profound side to Grant which the classic life of the colonial military officer failed to fulfil. Knowing that once he had completed ten years in the British army, he would be entitled to a gratuity, Grant invested his savings to date in an interest in a small fruit farm in the uplands not far from Nairobi. In 1925, after a second tour of duty in the north, he left the army, upped his agricultural investment with the gratuity, and from then on letters home came from Dixie Farm, Limuru.

The following year, 1926, was no less momentous for Grant than the one before had been. Pauline Buckeridge was travelling around Kenya with a friend from South Africa. With an introduction to his farming partner, a certain Corney Durham, the two girls motored up the farm drive one afternoon and straight into Grant's life. By the end of that year, he and Pauline were engaged, and six months later, Grant was on his way to Johannesburg to get married.

While Pauline was away in South Africa preparing for the wedding, Grant had built a cedar-panelled house in which to start their married life together - the Sheiling. This was just next door to the farm that was fast expanding into both dairy and tea. However, it had been clear from the start, at least to many of his family and friends, that the partnership with Durham was built on shaky ground, and the farm would not turn a profit for several more years to come. Tea can take three or four years from planting to first picking, and Grant was forced to supplement his income with hunting trips and building work. Guests and newly arrived son Guy kept them otherwise occupied, until, when Durham decided to throw his hat into the political arena, the sale of the farm became inevitable.

Sorely disappointed after having invested so much time, energy and money in the abortive project, and also perhaps at the realization that of his many abilities, good business sense was not one, in September 1929, Grant, wife and child sailed back to Britain. His family, most of whom had never met Pauline, were delighted to welcome her and young Guy to Scotland, leaving Grant to set off down the new career path of empire administrator. One of the requirements for joining the Colonial Service was for candidates to study law and administration for a year at university. So, while Pauline learnt about life in the Highlands, and gave birth to daughter Anne, her husband was being taught Swahili and the finer points of the English legal system at Magdalene College, Cambridge.

Grant was finished at Cambridge by the middle of 1930 and when asked back to Kenya to take up the post of District Officer in Mandera, on the Somali border, he jumped at the chance to get his foot on the bottom rung of the ladder of colonial administration. As with the location of many first appointments, this was no place to take a wife and children, and for Pauline the easiest option was to sit out his hardship posting with her parents in South Africa. Grant knew well how tough his accepting the offer would be on family life, but with a highly developed sense of public duty, he also knew that being apart from one another was a sacrifice they both had to make - and might well have to make again. In one of his typically thoughtful and affectionate letters to his wife, he wrote...

> I have made very many mistakes in the past; the one really sound thing I have done was to marry you, my dear one - you understand me better than anyone I know...I

am proud of you...who knows what service to a country, and to an ideal, means and who will help me serve as I should ... The past is over, and we must look forward. I know the family are glad that I have got this job - it is a pity that I took so long to get into the collar to work at it...If you really have to stay in South Africa, I suppose that it must be - it will be pretty hard to bear, but if it is for the good of the show that is the end of it...

Mandera was to be the start of 16 very successful years in Kenya (including wartime service in southern Abyssinia), culminating ultimately in his tragic and violent death as the District Commissioner in Narok. After Mandera, Grant had a short spell in Moyale, on the Abyssinian border, before being moved to Nyeri in the verdant foothills of the Aberdare Mountains, where Pauline joined him, soon to produce their third child, Deirdre. From there he enjoyed an equally friendly posting to Machakos, east of Nairobi. Following this he was sent back up north to control the arid wilderness around Moyale, the Italian invasion of Abyssinia, begun in October 1935, having put huge strains on the border.

Moyale was actually a much better base from which to operate than Mandera or Lodwar had been

- 'comfortable, healthy and has decent horses and one can get decent food'. Grant's primary responsibility was to keep the peace on the border, which was made particularly difficult by the Italians on the other side trying to arm the local tribesfolk against the Abyssinian government. His was more of a political than military task, and the success of his blend of diplomacy and derring-do was not lost on his superiors. By the outbreak of the Second World War in 1939 he had been promoted from District Officer to District Commissioner, now based at Kajiado in the Maasai Reserve, out on the plains east of Nairobi.

The reverberations of the outbreak of war were felt in very varying ways throughout Britain's colonies. With Italy joining the Axis alliance, Kenya's northern border became an even more dangerous frontier. As normally peaceful African neighbours were being urged to take up arms for opposing colonial causes, Grant found himself back in the Northern Frontier District, first as DC Wajir, then yet again in Moyale. Much as he must have agitated to return to active service, he was now too valuable for the Administration to lose. One of his most sensitive tasks was to form a group of 'Irregulars' from local tribesmen, who would scout and report back on Italian activities over the border. Grant was in what now appeared to be his element, 'far from the maddening crowd with lots of camel milk to drink and stars at night - even taking ones turn at sentry [duty] just as a precaution'.

With Haile Selassie back in Addis Ababa in April 1941, and the Italians ignominiously defeated, Grant was next asked to take on the post of Consul for Southern Abyssinia, based at Mega, just over the border. A lot of his time was spent in Addis Ababa playing the role of urban diplomat. In this, perhaps surprisingly, he seems to have felt quite at ease, provided there was some end in sight to the whole round of meetings, conferences and social engagements. He focused much of his energies on an attempt to obtain reparations for losses suffered by those on the Kenyan side of a very loosely demarcated border at the hands of Abyssinian tribesmen during the Italian occupation. His efforts were not in vain and some months later he was able to tell daughter Anne how 'the money I made the fuss about in Addis is to be paid to our people'.

By the end of the war Grant was back in a caretaker role, standing in for his friend Gerald Reece as acting Provincial Commissioner in Isiolo. There, where the foothills of Mount Kenya flatten out into the acacia-covered savannah of the north he found the climate much more amenable, but the work exhausting, not least because uncertainty surrounded his own future. He knew he was in line for posting to Narok as the District Commissioner there, but it was not until January 1946 that he was able to tell Pauline in Scotland how a colleague 'had been told positively that I am to go to Narok - so that, my dear, is our future fixed, I hope'.

Like so many others of his generation, what Grant really wanted above all else, after the cataclysmic upheavals of the war, was some stability in his life, which would allow him to settle down and unite his family. 'I long for Narok and to be at peace with you when this phase is all over, my dear' he wrote to Pauline from Isiolo, and a few days later he hoped that 'after a good few years in the desert we have arrived at a reasonable place in life and some degree of comfort'. As the time to move drew closer he told his daughter Anne, at school in England how '... it will be a great thrill to have Mummie back again and we shall go to Narok at the end of this week and take over from the Windleys'.

So they moved to Narok in March 1946. Excerpts from Pauline's letter to Anne, written the day after arriving on the 25th, give a feeling of the excitement they must have felt at driving together through the vastness of Africa to their new post and at the thought of at last settling down as a united family:

Here we are, having arrived yesterday about 4 o'clock...The road, a new Italian asphalt one, was lovely from Uplands [near Limuru] to the turn-off to come here [Maai Mahiu], cut out of the hills above the old one for about 20 miles, and then about 100 miles on here...

We saw lots of game. We both enjoyed the drive immensely as we had not done it previously, Suswa, Longonot and the other side of the Ngong Hills and masses of other ranges stretched before us - all very much Africa...

Our house is half a mile from the offices its a rough little *boma* [government enclave] and few people. I haven't gathered much about it yet. It's fun and Hugh and I are very, very happy and all that matters is to get settled in slowly and peacefully. We are surrounded by chests and all the bits and pieces of a home not unpacked...

The house is a nice one. One arrives on a terrace and up steps into a hall, used as a dining room with low big windows looking onto the garden...beds full of salvia, very blue, and snapdragons, Michaelmas daisies, penstemons and lots of other flowers and the lawn runs down to the summer house.

Not only did they both embrace the opportunity to live together after all the turmoil of the previous six years, but Grant would also have relished the new challenges and experiences the appointment offered. His assignments in the north had made him extraordinarily self-reliant, and having spent time in Kajiado, he already had some experience of administering a Maasai district. Indeed, it seems likely that his seniors saw the posting to Narok as a stepping stone to the highest administrative office of Provincial Commissioner.

Windley's Handing Over Report was finished by the end of March, and its 18 closely typed pages were awaiting Grant's arrival. It comprised a very comprehensive summary of the state of the Narok District from the Administration's perspective, which will have given Grant an idea of how best to focus his energies, as well as where he could expect trouble. An earlier crime wave down in Loliondo, on the Tanganyikan border, had resulted in the posting there of 20 tribal police who had recently rounded up 'wanted bad hats and some cattle stolen from the Kikuyu'; these latter [the Kikuyu], he reports later, had a 'tendency to settle on patches of forest and this should be watched and stopped'. East Coast fever and tsetse fly were continuing barriers to improving grazing availability, the report continued, local schools needed more supervision as well as better teachers, but the Narok hospital was flourishing.

Windley went on to recommend certain changes to the operation of the scheme for the government purchase of Maasai cattle, and with what, in hindsight, seems like uncanny prescience, described how 'the quota of 1,800 per sale is too high, particularly under recent serious drought conditions'.

Reading the report, Grant would have found the proposal to set up *moran* training camps the item on the incoming DC's extensive agenda most likely to absorb his time and attention. These were intended to 'supplement the indigenous system with more direct educative purposes, introducing some of our ideas on personal training and discipline to ensure bringing the young men of the tribe to hand under our guidance in the early stage of their moranhood'. Other topics covered in the report included the school of animal husbandry, roads, forests, mines and prisons. It ended with a list of relevant legislation and recommended background reading – amongst which was Joseph Thomson's 1883 *Through Masailand.*

Narok was all Grant and his wife could have hoped for. The District Commissioner's house – ten minutes' walk from the office – was surrounded by lawns and terraces, and looked out over ridges of scrub-covered hills. Their lives seemed to fit the cliché of working hard and playing hard - bouts of fishing, shooting, riding and entertaining between the grist of visits from other administrative officers and learning all about the district.

Absorbing the detail of administering 8,000 square miles was no easy task, and would have taken any new arrival a considerable time, but the work was well within Grant's capabilities. Support staff helped ease his way into the DC's chair by providing much needed continuity after Windley's departure. Writing to his parents in July, Grant explains how...

> Thanks to having Capt. Palmer, my temporary administrative assistant, we are more or less up to date and except for stores we are pretty well straight in the office. We shall have Bailward [A. N. Bailward, Officer in Charge, Maasai Extra-Provincial District] and Whitehouse here for the Local Native Council estimates meeting and [to discuss] the land for the School of Animal Husbandry. We have the nursing sister, and the policeman and his wife (who are leaving), his relief, and the policeman of the border patrol to supper tonight.

He ends by saying how 'We agreed last night as we got into bed that we were really quite indecently well fed and comfortable'.

One aspect of their lives that undoubtedly contributed to their self-contained contentment was the deeper spiritual commitment that they had both made just before the war. Their friends Gerald and Caroline Anderson had introduced them to the Oxford Group, soon to be renamed the Moral Re-Armament movement. Notwithstanding the demands it placed upon its members, the group's credo of 'absolute honesty, absolute purity, absolute unselfishness and absolute love' had immediately resonated with both of them. With its roots in Christianity, Grant and his wife found it more a way of life than a religion, and the total honesty between them was abundantly evident in their letters to each other. Such honesty is also sure to have pervaded Grant's attitude to his work and to those with whom he interacted. He had expressed to Pauline, shortly before they arrived in Narok, 'how much I need your love and support to live a really Christian life and to support me in doing my duty'.

Being particularly content with each other's company, they would not have bemoaned the paucity of European settlers around Narok. Hunting parties came by from time to time to collect permits, but most of the

Grants' daily fellowship was with other civil servants, many of whom lived in the *boma*. The local stores sold nothing but the most basic provisions and if Pauline wanted to stock up with anything remotely special, she had to visit Kijabe, the nearest railway station and around 100 miles east, or otherwise journey to the capital which was half as far again.

Pauline had planned a visit to Nairobi in early August, to see her dentist, as well as several friends, and no doubt to deal with any number of other social and domestic affairs. So, Monday, 12 August saw Grant and his wife having a midday glass of sherry and an early lunch. The meal finished and car loaded, they said what were unknowingly to be their last goodbyes to one another, and Pauline set off on the dusty dirt road to the capital, accompanied by their servant, Mohamed. From Narok, the road took her up and down a number of stream-valley switchbacks, before finally edging over the rim of the Great Rift Valley to reveal the gigantic crack in the earth's surface and vast expanse of plains below. In the hazy distance, she could probably make out the forested slopes of the far side, down which they had driven some four months earlier at the start of their renewed life together.

Photographs of Grant at the time show him as tall and slim with fair, thinning hair, invariably wearing spectacles and often a smile. He looks at ease with a life that his letters show he found both full and fulfilling. Now, with Pauline gone to Nairobi, and their three children, Guy, Anne and Deirdrie, all being schooled in England, there was no domestic interference with Grant's self-imposed work regime. He had repeatedly shown how well adapted he was to working on his own, and his wife's absence would at least allow him to catch up with any backlog of administrative chores.

A DC's lot involved extensive travel around his district, not least the better to know its inhabitants and their particular problems, and he had already marked Friday that week for purchasing cattle from the Maasai at Morijo in the heart of the Loita Hills. This would mean arriving there at least two days earlier to ensure enough cattle were actually produced for sale.

4

BUYING CATTLE

By 1946 history's most devastating conflict had just ended, and for both winners and losers food was in desperately short supply. Post-war Britain was to continue rationing meat until the middle of 1954, and in Kenya there were refugees, military personnel and former prisoners of war, as well as a fast expanding civilian population to feed. The war had highlighted the dangers of food insecurity and there was an assumption amongst the higher echelons of the Kenyan administration that not only should the colony be able to feed all its own inhabitants, but that there would also be a surplus for export to help ease the shortages in Britain and its empire.

So, in many districts, maximizing food production became central to good management. Africans owned over 95 per cent of the cattle in Kenya, and at the outbreak of the war, the Administration had introduced a quota system of compulsory purchase to try and divert some of the country's livestock wealth from the hoof to the tin.

Europeans had long perceived Maasai country to be seriously overstocked and attributed this to several different causes. Money was of little use to a Maasai; wealth and status were measured in cattle; and the extended Southern Maasai Reserve now accommodated both its original inhabitants - human and animal - as well as those resettled from the Northern Maasai Reserve following the 1911 Agreement. It was also apparent to some outside observers that the notion of communal tenure of land sat uneasily with the private ownership of the cattle that grazed that land. If there was no incentive to limit livestock numbers, was the degradation of pastures not inevitable?

Over and above the practicalities of cattle ownership as viewed by outsiders, the Maasai themselves would have added that cattle constituted a source of their own food as providers of milk and blood, as well as a medium of exchange with which to acquire other livestock. Beads, clothing and other cotton goods, non-meat food items, even wives could also be traded for livestock, rendering currency almost superfluous. More profoundly, the animals were accorded a near-sacred significance which defied most Europeans' understanding. This derived from the belief that on creating land and sky their god, *Enkai*, had given all cattle to the Maasai for safekeeping. So not only were cattle established as a link to God, but the Maasai, as the animals' custodians, were also set apart from, and above, all other tribes. They particularly contrasted themselves with agricultural communities who broke and tilled the soil, and in doing so destroyed the very grass on which the cattle depended for their grazing. Considering themselves the historic guardians of the world's cattle also helped provide the Maasai with a very convenient justification for stealing them from neighbours, on the grounds that by so doing they were merely restoring the animals to their rightful owners.

Another reason for the colonizers to encourage a reduction in African stock numbers was simply that, in theory at least, fewer cattle meant less likelihood of disease spreading amongst them. The energies of the Veterinary Department were principally focused on controlling rinderpest, East Coast fever and worst of all, contagious bovine pleuropneumonia. Related to measles, the rinderpest virus caused successive outbreaks of what was often a fatal disease, beginning with telltale signs of lost appetite, fever and discharges from eyes and nose. These outbreaks were usually brought under control through inoculation campaigns before the next one erupted. East Coast fever was a tick-borne disease, which could theoretically be subdued by dipping cattle, although the dipping facilities were often too distant from the remoter Maasai communities for them to bring in their animals as regularly as was required. Pleuropneumonia, or lungsickness, brought on coughing and breathing difficulties and was best combated by a combination of inoculation and quarantine. Yet no matter what the disease, confining large numbers of cattle in a restricted area not only increased the likelihood of it spreading within the herd, but also played havoc with the movement of animals and therefore any attempts to market them.

To a lot of veterinarians, it seemed clear that quarantine would inevitably lead to overstocking, and made no sense unless supported by intensive efforts to eradicate the particular disease responsible for the animals' confinement. On the other side of the fence sat the white farmers who generally argued for strict quarantine regulations to keep African cattle as far from their own as possible. Some of them also added the compulsory culling of surplus African stock into the equation, which then raised the whole question of how to process the carcasses.

For many years what had really held back the development of a vibrant Kenyan livestock trade, with or without contributions from the African herds, had been the absence of any meat processing plant. Whether cattle would have to be the subject of compulsory purchase or voluntarily offered for sale, without such facilities it was no use even contemplating a destocking scheme. When the government introduced a poll tax to help fund development expenditure, it proved almost impossible to collect, at least from the Maasai who could only have paid it by selling cattle.

The government first toyed with the idea of it being a fertiliser factory that would provide the most suitable end for the carcasses of surplus stock. Yet this failed to take account of the expectations of many of the settlers. They contended that Kenya should have its own meat export facilities to encourage them to invest in improving the quality of their livestock. This they were much less likely to do if the only market for their beef remained the domestic one.

With increasing pressure from both the European ranchers and the Administration, the government began to investigate the operations of the Liebig Company in Southern Rhodesia. The Director of Veterinary Services, Dr R Daubney and the rest of the delegation that was despatched down there returned much impressed by what they had seen. Liebig was not slow to take advantage of their enthusiasm, and wasted no time in sending its representatives up to Kenya. It took very little negotiation for the company to acquire land near the railway at Athi River, just east of Nairobi, together with a lease over ten thousand acres of bare plains as an adjacent holding ground. Apart from helping with loan financing, the colonial government also agreed to guarantee a steady enough throughput of livestock to justify Liebig's investment. To do so meant ensuring a regular contribution not only from the European ranchers but also from the huge African-owned cattle herds. This, in turn, would necessitate establishing some form of official purchase scheme and the creation of a wide-ranging network of stock routes, all converging on Athi River.

As soon as the Liebig factory opened in early 1938, it became clear that the supply of Kenyan cattle would fall far short of expectations. The prices were now much higher than when Liebig did its first costings, forcing the Administration to experiment with compulsory culling in Kamba country, not far from the factory. This began well, with plenty of cattle being offered for sale at prices the company could afford to pay, but enthusiasm for the scheme soon waned, and a march to Nairobi by a large number of Kamba demonstrators ultimately forced its abandonment. The government was then left with no option but to allow Liebig to source its stock elsewhere, and initially it was only thanks to a throughput of Tanganyikan animals that the cogs of its processors kept turning.

With the outbreak of the Second World War, there was a huge surge in the demand for tinned beef with which to feed Allied troops, and the Defence Regulations of 1939 gave the Kenya Supply Board sweeping powers to acquire livestock. These powers were delegated throughout the war, and beyond, jointly to the Livestock Control, which determined the relevant quotas, and to the Administration, which enforced them. A quota of 2,000 cattle a month was imposed on the Maasai as their contribution to the Allied forces' food supplies. The total was divided throughout the different sections of the tribe, and by 1946, for the Narok District this worked out at 1,800 per two months. Typically, DCs received requests for certain numbers of cattle from Livestock Control, which they then apportioned between the various tribal areas within their respective districts.

Leslie Whitehouse, affectionately know as 'Wouse' and famed in Kenya's colonial history as *Jomo's Jailor* (the title of his biography) was one of Grant's predecessors at Narok. He described in a taped interview how the practice was 'to allocate to each chief a quota of bullocks, calculated to be well within the capacity of his people to produce'. He then added that 'the Maasai were wholly cooperative and in due time the regular provision of slaughter bullocks became part of their wartime way of life'. What he also mentioned, though, was that many of the more wealthy and influential chiefs showed considerable reluctance to go along with the scheme, and 'thus it was that the whole business of estimating the quotas village by village and the selecting of the actual animals to be contributed by each family, and organizing the sales, required the personal presence of an administrative officer assisted by tribal police'.

Whether or not the Maasai actually were as obliging as Whitehouse suggests, if the scheme's success is measured in the numbers of cattle purchased, it undoubtedly fulfilled its purpose. And therein lay much of the problem. So many cattle had been bought during the war, that, no matter how cooperative the Maasai may have been when the scheme was first introduced, by the time Hugh Grant arrived in Narok in 1946, there was no doubting the reluctance which they felt in fulfilling the obligations imposed upon them. This reluctance was compounded by the fact that not only was the government the only buyer, it also determined the prices paid quite unilaterally. That the Maasai were well justified in feeling unfairly treated is clearly borne out by a comparison with the generally higher prices realised for comparable cattle by settler farmers, who were able to sell in a competitive market place.

Being hereditary healers and spiritualists, the Engedongi section of the Loita Maasai, who were responsible for providing many of the cattle Grant expected to purchase at the end of the week, exuded an air of superiority. They were notoriously unhelpful to outsiders and exerted powerful influences over their kinsmen, many of whom regarded them with suspicion, trepidation and sometimes jealousy. A chief of the neighbouring Purko section, which had earlier in the century been evicted from Laikipia, went so far as to suggest that all of them and their works should be placed into an extremely deep pit to which the earth should be returned with full speed. In 1945 the Engedongi had sent a message of defiance to the authorities saying they could not produce their cattle quota that year, and twelve months later their reluctance to cooperate had not abated.

***

So an uneasy tension pervaded the Morijo area of the Loita Hills. It would have been no surprise if Grant felt somewhat apprehensive as his Bedford truck headed away from the DC's corrugated iron-roofed house and down past the administrative offices to join the main road over the Narok river. A few miles further on he met the *Ewaso Nyiro* (dark river) and just after that, turned left to drive for an hour or so across the Loita Plains. As a committed hunter, was he mentally measuring the horns of some of the game animals he passed? There were wildebeest on these flatlands - a resident population that never joined the migrating millions moving back and forth within the Mara-Serengeti ecosystem. Zebra and ostrich also grazed there, and having lived in East Africa for the best part of 25 years, he had probably smiled often enough at the gazelles he also saw which bore his own name. Grant's gazelle were so called after his namesake and fellow Scotsman, James Augustus Grant, who in 1860 had accompanied John Hanning Speke in search of the source of the Nile.

If Grant encountered Maasai cattle, grazing whatever they could find in the dry bush, he would surely have recalled Windley's words that 'the quota of 1,800 per sale is too high, particularly under recent serious drought conditions'. The difficulty in getting quotas to match availability of cattle led to continual disagreements between the Livestock Control that set them and those on the ground whose duty it was to collect the animals to fill them. Windley had gone on to tell Grant that he would need to 'accept a certain shortfall philosophically as no one agrees if you suggest a reduction in quota'. So Grant must have looked over any herds he saw on his way, not only to assess their general condition but also to see if there were many good bullocks amongst them capable of contributing to future sales. Might he even have stopped to talk to the herdsmen? As well as his camp staff he probably had tribal policemen in the truck with him able to translate from Maasai, which Grant wouldn't understand, to Swahili, which he could speak well.

It was dry that August throughout Narok District and the cattle in the lowlands were probably faring worse than those up in the hills. As Grant bumped across the plains his wheels spun up a trail of fine dust behind him. Clumps of tall, spiky aloes, aromatic *leleshwa* bushes, and whistling thorns, with ant-inhabited galls at the end of their branches, fringed the road. With it having rained so little, he would have had few concerns about negotiating the steep road ahead of him, which he had to follow to reach Morijo. This wound its way up the side of the distant hills he could just make out in the blue haze, their outline sharpening as he approached the cluster of huts comprising the settlement of Naroosura.

From Naroosura the road crossed the river of that name, and then followed a tributary stream up its valley. Strangler figs and other taller trees began to take over from the stunted vegetation of the flatlands. Then, leaving the river valley, the track zigzagged up the open hillside before levelling out among the high ground's mosaic of forest and clearings, where buffalo often grazed. If Grant allowed his thoughts to drift beyond the road in front of him, they might have moved on to the work awaiting him at his destination - the collecting pens at Morijo.

To these he hoped the Engedongi Maasai would be bringing their cattle the following day. If not, he would need to use the authority vested in him to requisition cattle in order to make up the quotas.

Regulation 50 of the 1939 Defence Regulations empowered the Kenya Supply Board to requisition cattle if insufficient numbers were willingly offered for sale. The Maasai as a whole had been generally cooperative in their voluntary submission of animals during the war years and while Grant may not have appreciated it at the time, these powers of requisition were actually little used. In his evidence at Karambu's trial, Bailward, as the prosecution's thirteenth witness, explained how the whole system worked, informing the court that...

> In present time requisitioning in the Maasai Reserve has been in force to a very limited extent. 123,081 cattle have been sold to the Livestock Control by the Maasai, from June 1940 to December 1945. It would be a matter of surprise to me if more than 500 of these cattle had been requisitioned. The others have been brought in by the Maasai without requisitioning or undue pressure. They did it to help the war effort and in doing so behaved extremely

well. I get a [request] from government for a certain number of cattle. The quota is divided among the various sections. The DC appraises the sections of the quota they have to supply. If a section fails to comply then in very rare cases we are driven to requisition the cattle direct.

Buyers employed by Livestock Control attended the sales to do the actual valuing and purchasing of the cattle. William Munro was one such, having graduated from assistant to buyer more than five years earlier. On the same day that Pauline left for Nairobi, Grant had spoken with him, asking for his help at the Morijo sale. Munro had therefore set aside the last three days of the week, and by the time the buyer's lorry pulled up at the Morijo campsite near the Veterinary Department cattle pens on Wednesday afternoon, he found Grant already settled into his own chosen resting place some two miles away. After putting up his tents, Munro, as he would describe in the sworn statement he made at the preliminary inquiry into Grant's death, 'visited his [Grant's] camp at his request and we talked generally about cattle collecting, etc. until I left for my own camp at about 9.00 p.m.'

By the standards of the day, and the region, Morijo was a busy centre with an enormous catchment area.

It was essentially the hub of livestock activity, the Veterinary Department having installed a cattle crush and dipping facilities a few hundred yards up from the *Olchorro Onyokie* river. Morijo also hosted the first elementary 'outschool' (as the Administration described it) in the Loita Hills. With such pupils as their fathers would reluctantly surrender to the dubious benefits of education coming from far and wide, this was unavoidably a primitive boarding facility.

Each boy's family was required to contribute a cow to cover the term's costs of his stay in the children's village. The pupils were taught the 'three Rs', and also learned the rudiments of animal husbandry, knowledge of which was supposed to help them improve the quality of their families' livestock once they got back home.

A 'river' might be stretching the definition of the *Olchorro Onyokie* headwaters, but it was close to being a permanent watercourse, edged with tall acacia trees whose shade created several ideal campsites. Grant had avoided camping in the immediate area of the cattle pens, where there was always a bustle of Maasai activity, and so most likely chose to make his base on the edge of one of the several smaller stream beds which joined up with the river. He also needed somewhere to which his lorry could be easily driven and equipment unloaded for at least a two-day stay.

While Grant clearly hoped that the Maasai would volunteer cattle to fill their quota, his expectations may have been more realistic, and the next day the omens for an easy sale were not good. If Friday's proceedings were to run smoothly, cattle should already have been arriving the day before, Thursday, and they were not. Grant visited Munro's camp in the morning but for the rest of the day appears to have been busy with other administrative duties, including measuring out sites for more stores in Morijo. The whole time he must have been keeping an uneasy eye on the collecting pens to see if they were filling up and by late afternoon he would have known that no cattle were to be forthcoming. The shortfall would need rounding up by him and his *askaris* [guards] at daybreak the next morning.

As he turned in that evening Grant knew he would be getting very little sleep. It appeared that not a single animal had been brought in voluntarily, and if he was going to collect up cattle the next morning, he had to reach their enclosures well before they were driven out for the day's grazing. So he roused himself before 1.00 a.m., after what cannot have been more than three hours sleep, no doubt cursing the intransigence of the Engedongi Maasai that was forcing him to use his powers to requisition their animals. He would have needed all his ancestral Scottish insensitivity to the cold as he pulled on first a blue shirt, then a khaki one before topping them both with a green pullover and tucking in a silk scarf. Long trousers, socks and sandals had to keep his lower half warm, and picking up hat and glasses he emerged from his tent into the blackness and headed for his lorry.

Maasai tribal policeman, Tigane ole Karmusho, watched Grant setting off, affirming at the preliminary inquiry how, 'At 1.00 a.m...Major Grant's lorry with him in it drove to Mr Munro's camp and he and Mr Munro and some police went off in Mr Munro's lorry down the Loliondo road.' Tigane then described how, while Grant and Munro had headed off in their own direction, he 'and other police went off on foot to requisition cattle from some *bomas* nearby on Major Grant's orders', adding that he, Tigane, had been given this order 'as cattle had not been brought in for the cattle sale to Livestock Control'.

At the same inquiry, Munro related the start of that fateful day, from his own perspective:

Major Grant woke me up at 1.40 a.m. telling me that he was going out to collect cattle and asking for two *askaris* of his who should have been in my camp. We woke up my camp and found one of them. He then asked me to send some of my staff to some *bomas* [in this sense, cattle enclosure] nearby... and I did so. He and I then went off in my lorry with his *askaris* and a certain number of my staff. We went along the road to Loliondo for about ten miles and then turned off and went about another two miles into the bush, guided by members of the DC's staff. We came to a Maasai *manyatta*. Now we were about 12 miles from my camp. We arrived here at about 4.30 a.m. Major Grant posted three men round this *boma* with instructions that no cattle were to be allowed out till his return. We then went on to a second *manyatta* about a mile away. More men were posted round this *manyatta* too, with instructions not to let any cattle out. Major Grant then asked me the time and I told him it was 5 o'clock.

We waited there till nearly 6 o'clock when two Maasai came out of the *boma*... Major Grant and I then entered the *boma* just at daylight, and I was instructed by Major Grant to select 20 of the best bullocks. I did so with his assistance and of our men. We took more than 20 outside and eventually selected 19, others having been returned on the request of various elders from that *manyatta*. The 19 selected animals were sent on ahead with our men to the other *manyatta*, Major Grant and I walking behind. On arrival at the other *manyatta* [the Sendeu *manyatta*] Major Grant told me to select the best bullocks without stating a number. We selected nine, making a total of 28. I cannot tell definitely why these cattle were being requisitioned but I know that Major Grant was very cross with that section of the Maasai and that cattle should have been brought in there on the 15th and none had arrived at all.

The other crucial witness to the requisitioning from the second *manyatta* was Karambu's oldest brother, Ranan ole Sendeu, who was on the supply side of the cattle equation and gave affirmed evidence at his brother's trial:

Early that morning I was at the *manyatta* and Accused was at *ol pul* [meat camp]. That morning Major Grant and Mr Munro came to the *manyatta* and selected cattle. They said they were selecting as the cattle were late in coming in. We had received no previous information. All the Loita cattle had not been collected...It was usual for the Loita location to supply a certain number of cattle to government and to be paid for them. When Major Grant and Mr Munro requisitioned the cattle nobody protested. This was about 6 a.m. They took nine cattle from our *manyatta*. Accused's bullock was amongst the nine. It was a very big black bullock with long horns. There were about 200 cattle in the *manyatta*.

Seven of the nine cattle were provided by the Sendeu family, the remaining two by other elders. These were added to the first batch of 19, and all 28 ordered to be driven by the *askaris* to the Veterinary Department collecting pens, a journey that would be likely to get them there around mid-morning. Munro and Grant then went on ahead, doubtless relieved to have concluded that part of the exercise, and returned to Munro's camp. There they had coffee, Grant smoked a cigar and as he left the two agreed to rendezvous at the pens for the sale at 11.00.

There was only the one main road through the southern end of the Loita Hills, and Grant had travelled the first part on Wednesday on his way from Narok to Morijo. From there the road continued on to Entesekera and into what was then Tanganyika to

Loliondo. In the early morning darkness, Grant and Munro had turned from Morijo onto the main road, starting off down towards Tanganyika before heading left up into the valley occupied by the Engedongi section. Having selected their cattle and returned from the *manyattas* to Munro's camp for coffee, it was left to the tribal *askaris* to drive the cattle down the wide open plains that lead to Morijo and the collecting pens.

By the time Grant and Munro met up to begin the sale, the 28 animals had just arrived and were being herded into the large holding enclosure. This was fenced around with thorn branches and from it, cattle were being released in small groups into the triangular post and rails collecting pen. Munro outlined the procedure:

> When the cattle are brought into the collecting pen, I examine them individually, decide on their value, write the value on a purchase ticket in triplicate, call out the value to Major Grant on his instructions, and hand over the two copies of the ticket to the owner standing against the rails through the First Grade *Askari* Tigane.

Tigane himself added his own details, describing at the trial how he was 'in the pen when Mr Munro was valuing and buying the animals. Mr Munro was writing some tickets and handing them to me. I searched for the owner of the tickets when given to me. When I found the owner I gave him the ticket and he went to the clerk.' If the Maasai had trouble understanding how much their animals had fetched, Grant would then, through a Swahili-speaking Maasai elder, Katina ole Legei, help the owners read the tickets. Thus enlightened, they went off to the clerks, who were sitting behind desks in Munro's lorry, and exchanged each of the tickets for cash.

While its owner was being paid his cash, the animal that a few hours earlier had been part of his herd was moved on from the collecting pen to the narrow crush to be branded. There the searing iron on hairy hide provided the final proof that ownership had now been transferred to the Colony and Protectorate of Kenya.

In all, there were 58 cattle to be valued and sold that day, the other 30 having also been requisitioned by tribal police from *manyattas* closer to Morijo, at the same time as Grant and Munro were selecting their 28. The quality was good, not only since they had, of necessity, selected many of the animals themselves, but also because the Engedongi had held back beasts from previous sales. Their condition showed there was clearly enough grazing still to be found, despite both the alleged overstocking and the near drought conditions that had prevailed in much of the District during the first half of the year. (The total rainfall for 1946 in the Narok government *boma*, where anything less than 20 inches was considered a bad year, would end up at 18).

Munro's valuations were much higher than at previous Morijo sales - up 30 per cent to around five pounds an animal. This was due not only to the better quality but also to the government having just increased cattle prices. Grant realised that the higher payments might help soften the Engedongi's reluctance to cooperate in future sales. He was therefore particularly anxious that these increased prices received as much ringside publicity as possible.

As the buying began, Grant may already have been calculating whether he would be finished in time to pack up camp and get back home before dark. According to Munro, 'Major Grant asked me to start buying as soon as possible as he wished to get back to Narok as he was very busy. I began buying immediately at about 11.15 to 11.30.' Needing to requisition cattle had set their timing back several hours. Having been up since one in the morning, Grant was in no mood to pay much attention to a young man who began to remonstrate over the inclusion amongst the cattle being sold of a fine black bullock with large horns and a white tip to its tail.

5

THE SPEAR IS THROWN

Karambu ole Sendeu had not been at home to protest the removal of his favourite animal amongst the nine beasts provided by his *manyatta*; and surprisingly, nor had any of his family demurred on his behalf, and this included his brother Ranan. Had Karambu been there, he would have explained to Grant and Munro in the cold light of dawn, how its mother had died soon after giving birth, and how he had brought up the calf, which he had named Lemelelu after its mother, like his own child. Had he been there, this story would never have unfolded in the tragic manner that it had begun to on that early Loita morning.

Three days earlier, Karambu, his full brother Letoile, second to Ranan, (Karambu being the youngest of the three full siblings), and cousin Merepari ole Topoti - all now having passed through their *eunoto* ceremony and moved from *moran* to junior elder - had gone off together into an *ol pul*. Their usual food in the *manyatta* was milk and blood, and with it being taboo for women to witness warriors, or even junior elders consuming meat, this was usually eaten some distance away from the homestead.

There they stayed together, living off the flesh of the animal they had slaughtered, perhaps glad to be away from the chores of *manyatta* life, responsible only to one another. As well as eating meat, they most likely made up soups, laced with roots, stems and leaves of forest herbs that they collected up themselves. They were all to emerge from the meat camp speaking easily to one another. Presumably therefore, Karambu lived up to the better side of his reputation for only losing his temper for good reason, and in none of the evidence is it suggested that the three days at the *ol pul* were not spent in easy companionship. Much of the time would have been characterized by inactivity, with alternating bouts of eating, sleeping and talking. The days might have been enlivened by songs, chants and dances, as well as by physical contests of strength and agility. Karambu's colleagues would recall him greasing his spear - as they all did - probably with the fat of the animal they were eating, adding that this was merely a protective measure against rust and no indicator of any likelihood of the weapon's immediate use.

As a young boy Karambu probably carried with him a wooden stick, sharpened like a spear, while he tended the sheep and goats. Later he may have carried his father's spear, but had to await circumcision before receiving his own. This would have remained his most treasured possession for the rest of his life, however long that might be. While a *moran*, Karambu and his fellow warriors held many competitions to see which of them could throw his spear furthest, or most accurately. Moving on from moranhood, he would have remained inseparable from his spear, and the more blood it had shed, the greater his pride in the weapon.

There were several different spear designs from which a *moran* could choose, although they all consisted of the same three basic parts, an upper iron blade, central wooden shaft and lower iron point. Munro would later describe Karambu's spear as having 'a shortish medium-brown handle'. The fact that it was able to pass right through a human torso certainly meant it had no protrusions at the bottom of what must have been a long, narrow blade, making it most likely to be of the design known as *empere sero* – *empere* meaning 'spear', and *sero*, 'brown', referring to the colour of the blade.

On the Friday morning Letoile left the others in the *ol pul* camp, and on reaching his *manyatta*, learned about the cattle requisitioning. In haste he turned back to meet Karambu and Merepari, by now both also on their way home. Having passed on the news, the other two delegated Merepari to return and look after the children in the *manyatta*, probably collecting them up to take back to the *ol pul* for their share of the remains of the meat. Letoile and Karambu meanwhile, set off on the trail of their requisitioned cattle to the Morijo collecting pen. They moved quickly over the ground with long, loping Maasai strides, spears over their shoulders or clasped at the point of balance by extended arms hanging down their sides. Giving evidence, Letoile remembered that on the walk to join their cattle 'the Accused said he was going to beg for his bullock from the *bwana* [boss]'. This was hardly surprising. Not only was Karambu inordinately fond of the animal, but, as he would explain at his trial, he had no other bullocks left, only ten cows. What was surprising though, was Letoile's further assertion that his brother 'was not angry at all'.

Letoile's memory may have let him down at the trial, and perhaps his brother was in fact starting to become agitated on the way to the collecting pen. Whether he was or not, once Karambu reached Morijo, and there saw the animal on which he had focused so much affection over the years, there can be little doubting the emotions that then began to overtake him. The sale was well underway and crowds of young Maasai men were milling noisily around the enclosures. Prices were being called out and cash was changing hands. Grant, wearing hat and glasses, leant on the rails, smoking one of his cigars. Speaking in Swahili, he explained to the owners, through his Maasai interpreter, Katina, how much their cattle had sold for. While in Karambu's mind, Lemelelu remained the object of his deep affection, in reality, having reached the collecting pen with the other 27 animals, his bullock was now one of a random herd, united no longer by common ownership or ancestry, but by suitability for slaughter.

Letoile and Karambu split up when they arrived, Letoile heading for the rails and losing track of his brother. Ranan had reached the collecting pen before the other two, and never saw either of them arrive. Later, when the time came for him to give evidence at his brother's trial, he explained how, when he first noticed Karambu...

'He had his spear, exhibit 3, with him. I saw the Accused's black bullock sold. I received the ticket from Mr Munro with the ticket price on it. I received it, as I am head of the *manyatta*. The cattle are first in the big *boma*, then driven into the collecting pen, three or four at a time, and after being valued and bought they are driven outside and branded. Before the Accused's ox had been branded, Accused went up and spoke to Major Grant. I was near enough to hear what was said. Accused begged Major Grant to return his one bullock. He spoke to Major Grant in Maasai and pointed to the bullock. Major Grant shook his head. I heard Major Grant saying *hapana* [no]. Major Grant leaned against the rails of the buying pen. He continued to read out the prices.

In response to later questions, Ranan added that, 'At the time he was speaking to Major Grant he [Karambu] was happy as he thought the bullock would be returned to him. After Major Grant said *hapana*, the Accused still pleaded with him and still appeared to be happy. Major Grant kept on saying *hapana*.'

The Maasai owners of requisitioned cattle were wont to complain that they had never received any prior notice of the regular quota requirements, and quite likely Karambu advanced this argument in what must have been an increasingly agitated request. He may also have tried to explain, in Maa, how this was the only bullock he had left. After selling 25 other beasts to the government during the war, and five more during the previous eight or nine months, all that now remained in his herd were cows. However it may have been, many onlookers heard Grant conclude the exchange with an emphatic, final, Swahili *'hapana'* - 'no' - before turning to continue reading out the prices for the next batch.

Grant's own thought process at the time is not hard to imagine. As far as he was concerned, the young man's *manyatta* had been given adequate notice to select animals to fulfil its quota and bring them to Morijo the previous day. This they had not done. Notwithstanding Karambu's family having ignored the orders of the Administration, they had still been given every chance to contest the requisitioning of specific animals earlier in the morning, as others had done. (Munro specifically mentions in his evidence how he and Grant had 'eventually selected 19, others having been returned on the request of various elders.') This they had not done either. And then even when the 28 cattle were nearing the collecting pens in mid-morning, Grant had, according to Munro at the trial...

> informed me that he had allowed the Maasai to take one more bullock, a brindled bullock out of the stock. He mentioned the name of the man, Simel, one of the *laibon* clan from whom these cattle were being requisitioned from the second *manyatta* we visited and from which 19 cattle were taken.

Karambu had missed all three opportunities, and now he was asking for his bullock back even after it had already been valued and the ticket issued to his brother. On top of that, Grant had been up since before one in the morning, and was hoping to get back to Narok later in the day.

So, Karambu retreated, away from the District Commissioner and the ringside bustle into his own world. Perhaps he watched Lemelelu's branding, surely the final and irreversible act to seal the loss of his animal to a colonial cause for which he had scant respect. In his statement, he admitted how, 'When I was refused my animal back I stood and thought about it and it was then that my mind went wrong and I was as in darkness and overtaken by madness'. However long he remained with his thoughts – Munro suggested 20 minutes elapsed between his valuing Lemelelu and Grant's death – it was long enough to damn any defence that his killing Grant was a spontaneous reaction to provocation by the District Commissioner.

What exactly was going through Karambu's mind as he brooded under his black cloud? The '*hapana*' was central to the exchange between him and Grant, and Karambu could have taken it in many different ways. Did he truly understand what Grant meant, or did he load it with much more significance than the DC ever intended, and build it up into a personal insult? It was certainly emphatic, a put down, and a refusal to take the matter any further. It was also a refusal without any accompanying explanation, which may have made it appear doubly damning.

That Karambu was losing his favourite bullock was bad enough, but why did he love it so much? What other sentiments weighed upon him? All that emerged in the trial was that Karambu had brought up the calf after its mother died; but Maasai are well used to raising orphaned animals, so why was Lemelelu really so treasured? Were there other reasons which, with their lack of any common language, neither Grant at the collecting pen nor his lawyer at the trial, were able to elicit from Karambu? Was it perhaps Lemelelu's mother or even her mother, that was actually so treasured. Did Karambu steal the mother on a cattle raid, and so regard her offspring as a symbol of his own bravery? Did he have to stick-fight with one of his fellow *moran* to determine who would take the cow, after they both claimed it in the heat of an attack on a neighbouring tribe? Was it the only cow he captured on a raid, or was the mother herself a descendant of a beast seized by his own father? Any one or more of these thoughts might have loomed large as his mood darkened.

While Karambu agonised over his loss, Munro continued to assess the qualities of the individual animals, walking in among them in the collecting pen, valuing first one and then the other, writing three separate tickets for each as he did so. As Munro moved around the cattle, Katina continued translating for Grant, who was still standing just outside the pen, his arms resting along the top rail. One of Katina's own cattle had just been valued, having also been amongst those requisitioned, and realizing he had forgotten to remove the bell from its neck, he began unsheathing his knife to cut the thong from which the bell was suspended.

As Katina concerned himself with removing the bell, Munro continued to concentrate on the remaining cattle, his back to Grant. Suddenly, out of nowhere, as if long ago separated from the arm that threw it, a spear slithered across the dusty, trampled ground of the collecting pen in front of Munro. It was followed almost immediately by a young Maasai man, who leapt into the pen, picked up the weapon, and then clambered out the other side. A few seconds later, two more young Maasai jumped into and out of the pen, obviously in pursuit of the first, causing Munro to climb up onto the rails to watch the chase. Then he looked round for Grant, and could not see him.

The first Maasai was Karambu; the other two were his brothers.

While Munro had become aware of the spear before having any idea of the injury it had caused, Ranan had a more removed perspective. He had seen enough to know both that it was Karambu who had thrown the spear and that Grant had been his target. In his statement, he related how...

> I looked round and saw *bwana* on the ground. I also saw [my brother] the Accused jumping into the small *boma*. I also saw him bending to enter the big *boma* from the small *boma*. I then saw him picking up a spear and holding it upraised. I saw him running to jump over the big *boma*. I went outside that *boma* and by the time I got out of it, the Accused had reached the bush. I chased and caught him. On catching him my *shuka*, exhibit 2, got caught in his spear. On catching him Letoile came up to help me. I point him out. He is my full brother. I questioned Accused. 'Why did you do such a big thing as this?' He said he was caught by madness. I asked him why he had done it and he said he had been refused the bullock. He mentioned the animal. He said

the DC had refused to give him the bullock. He said he had speared the DC. I took the Accused back to the crush and I handed him to an *askari*. I said to the *askari* 'take him and shoot him'. The Accused agreed...

Back at the collecting area, it was only after Munro had come down from the rails, crossed the pen and clambered up the other side, that he then saw Grant, by now some 15 feet from the pen, face down on the ground. Munro recalled at the inquest that 'He was wearing a hat and it was partly off his head...He was wearing glasses and these were up on his forehead'. At least two minutes had passed since the spear had slithered across the earth in front of the cattle buyer, during which time all the Maasai, other than some of the tribal policemen, had taken collective fright and disappeared.

Munro continued. 'I turned him over and the first thing I noticed was blood coming from his mouth. I then took his head in my left arm and realised he was dying or dead.' He then called over one of the clerks and the two of them pulled up Grant's shirts and jersey to reveal a wound around the heart. Grant was dead, pierced by a spear thrown with such force that it had gone right through his body - into his back and out the other side - exiting where the sixth rib joins the breastbone, before sliding, bloodied, across the ground of the collecting pen. Having been leaning against the rails when he was speared, and yet found by Munro some distance from the pen, suggests Grant must have dragged himself soundlessly across the ground before expiring. Ranan was the only one to admit to seeing him collapse, but he had set off in immediate pursuit of his brother, and in their anxiety to escape the scene of such an indefensible event, none of the other Maasai remained to witness what happened next after the District Commissioner fell.

After pouring water over Grant's head and chest, Munro called for his own camp bed on which to stretcher the body to his lorry. He then saw the two pursuers, Ranan and Letoile, escorting back their brother, who he ordered to be handcuffed. None of the three brothers carried a spear, although the weapon that had killed Grant was handed over to Munro shortly afterwards, having been dropped on the ground by Ranan as they returned. Tribal police then loaded Karambu into Munro's lorry, and the killer and his victim, the living and the dead, travelled back to Narok together.

The party reached the Administration headquarters around 4.15 p.m. where Grant's body was handed over by a tribal policeman to the local medical officer, W. E.

Lawes. The doctor attested later that he immediately recognised the body on which he was to carry out a post-mortem examination that same evening. His report concluded that 'death was due to haemorrhage and shock consequent upon a wound caused by a sharp stabbing instrument which has completely penetrated the body'.

Grant's body was flown the next day, Saturday, to Nairobi, to be buried on Sunday, with full military honours, on the Ngong Hills. His grave backed onto the hills, whose tops at the time of the funeral were hidden in the mists of a Kenyan highland August. Below, the great sweep of the Athi plains stretched out far into the distance. Hugh was the third of his parents' sons to die in the service of King and Country within the space of four years, following Frank, killed at Tobruk in 1942, and James in Tunisia a year later. Born on 22 January 1897, Hugh Murray Grant had died in Kenya's Loita Hills on 16 August 1946.

On the commemorative bronze plaque which marks the grave were inscribed these words from the New Testament's Epistle to the Hebrews - 'Faith is the substance of things hoped for - the evidence of things not seen'.

**

In the Kenya Gazette of 3 September 1946, an obituary for Hugh Grant appeared as Government Notice No. 776:

> His Excellency the Governor deeply regrets to announce the death at Narok in the Maasai District on 16 August 1946, of Major Hugh Grant, MBE, MC, as the result of a spear wound.
>
> The late Major Grant first came to Kenya in 1921 on secondment to the King's African Rifles from his own regiment, the Queen's Own Cameron Highlanders. He joined the Administration in July 1930, and the greater part of his service as an Administrative Officer was spent in the Northern Frontier District.
>
> During the recent war Major Grant was largely responsible for the formation of the unit of irregulars which became known as 'Grant's Irregulars' and he served with that unit in the campaign in the Northern Frontier District and Abyssinia.
>
> On the conclusion of the campaign in East Africa he was appointed as District Commissioner at Moyale and subsequently as HBM Consul for Southern Ethiopia at Mega.

Major Grant was a man of outstanding character whose courage, generosity and great personal charm endeared him to all those of his brother officers who had the pleasure of serving with him. By his death the government has lost an officer of great worth and rare qualities who will be sadly missed by his many friends.

Major Grant is survived by a widow, a son, and two daughters to whom, on behalf of the government, His Excellency extends his sincere sympathy.

6

THE TRIAL AND ITS AFTERMATH

Karambu, meanwhile, was remanded in custody until the preliminary inquiry into a charge of murder, held at Narok on 23 August before First Class Magistrate R. E. Wainwright. The purpose of the inquiry was to ascertain whether there was sufficient evidence to commit the Accused, who was unrepresented, for trial before His Majesty's Supreme Court of Kenya. The inquiry effectively comprised written depositions from the most crucial witnesses in support of the prosecution's case - various police officers, Lawes, Munro, Ranan and Letoile, and Maasai elder, Katina ole Legei. Exhibits included a plan of the crime scene, a spear, clothing, the post-mortem report and a medical report on Karambu in which he was simply 'certified fit'.

When his turn came, Karambu called no witnesses but opened his evidence with almost touching simplicity:

> This trouble occurred over the requisi-
> tioning of a bullock of mine which I par-

ticularly loved. I asked the DC himself at the sale when he was watching the sale and he refused to give it back. I had thought that he would return it when I asked but when he did not do so I became very angry indeed and so killed him. I am saying the truth when I say that not a single person actually saw me kill him for everyone at the time was watching the sale. I did this because I loved the bullock much more than others for its mother had died young and I had to rear it as though it was my own child. The spear passed right through and went on into the thorn *boma* so I followed it, picked it up and ran off with it. My brothers chased me and Ranan caught me. But I was not running hard and if he had not caught me I should myself have returned and given myself up. That is what I have to say of the crime I have committed.

The magistrate certified that Karambu's evidence was 'taken in my presence and hearing and contains accurately the whole evidence given by the accused person. It was made in the Maasai language and translated into Swahili by Court Interpreter Sendura and [from Swahili] into English by me to the best of my knowledge and skill'.

With Karambu not denying he had killed Grant, and Munro, along with Karambu's brothers and other Maasai present at the collecting pen all giving detailed evidence of the events leading up to the fatal spear throw, it was no surprise when Wainwright concluded 'I consider the evidence sufficient to put the accused person Karambu ole Sendeu on his trial, and therefore commit him for trial to the Supreme Court on a charge of murder Contra Section 198 [Penal Code]'.

Karambu's trial began two weeks later, on 10 September, in the Maasai Council Hall at Narok. The importance the government attached to Criminal Case 150 of 1946 was emphasized by the appointment as the presiding judge of Chief Justice Sheridan, whose arrival the previous day had been marked by his first inspecting a guard of honour of 16 police constables. Mr H. E. Stacey represented the Crown and Mr J. A. Burke appeared for the defence. As was then the practice, the judge was assisted by three independent Maasai assessors, whose role was akin to that of an advisory jury. Almost always drawn from an accused's own community, as they were in this case, the assessors helped ensure that decisions of fact made by a court, which was inevitably presided over by a European judge, were informed by the customs and codes of the society to which an accused belonged.

The trial appears to have caused considerable excitement amongst Karambu's peers, the *East African Standard* reporting how 'several natives had waited from the early hours to witness the proceedings and before long there was a crowd of several hundred. The small court house was packed and others took up positions of vantage at the open windows.' Karambu himself seemed undaunted by the arcane and intimidating process of the English criminal justice system as practised in the Colony and Protectorate of Kenya. The *Standard* recorded that 'The central figure of the drama, Accused himself, appeared the least perturbed. For the most part he sat on the stone floor, playing with his toes and idly toying [with] the fawn-coloured blanket, which served as his cloak'.

When formally charged in court Karambu replied, 'I did not kill him on purpose', which Sheridan accepted as a plea of 'not guilty'. However, production of the Accused's spear as one of the exhibits, together with damning evidence from Munro, Karambu's brothers and several others, left little chance for surprise revelations. With the fact of Karambu having killed Grant being beyond dispute, his lawyer Burke was left with little option but to focus any chance of a successful defence either on his client's state of mind at the time or on trying to establish the provocative nature of the victim's behaviour.

The prosecution called a total of 15 witnesses, four from the Administration - Mills, Munro, Lawes and Bailward - and the remainder all local Maasai other than Assistant Police Inspector James Mutisya Mathome. As successive Maasai witnesses appeared to give evidence for the prosecution, Burke, for the defence, began to tease out repeated references to a history of epilepsy in Karambu's family, as well as possibly in Karambu himself. Under cross-examination, Lawes, who had also conducted the post-mortem on Grant, explained how he had examined the Accused both on the day after the incident and, more carefully, a week later. He referred to evidence of a hysterical fit which Karambu had experienced as a *moran*, although muting the potential value of this revelation to the defence by adding that he felt it took more than one fit to sustain a history of epilepsy.

Various brothers and age mates also supported the epileptic incident, including Ranan, who told how he was present when his brother had the fit. 'He was attacked suddenly, we caught hold of him and poured water on him. He shook his head and fell over. It lasted a short time.' However, Ranan's evidence was not entirely helpful to his brother's cause either, because he added that Karambu 'did not have an epileptic fit the day Major Grant was killed.' Letoile also spoke about how he himself never had an epileptic fit nor to his knowledge did Ranan. 'Accused has had one about three years ago, perhaps before the recently concluded war. He has had only one to my knowledge.'

Several witnesses made reference to Karambu's father, Sendeu, whose death from epilepsy seemed almost to have entered local Maasai folklore. Clearly the cause of much administrative concern, his suspected involvement in local tribal insurrections was reason for Sendeu's deportation out of the area around 1923 to Meru, where he spent nearly four years. Katina, the elder from the adjoining *manyatta* who had been helping Grant translate prices shortly before his death, suggested that Sendeu's wife was actually pregnant with Karambu when he was deported. Katina himself had known Sendeu, describing him as 'a big man in Maasai'. He then filled in more of Sendeu's background. 'He was son of Lenana and grandson of Mbatian. Lenana was a paramount chief of Maasai. Sendeu was a *laibon* who was deported to Meru. I don't know if Accused was born. Sendeu came back to Maasai land. I don't know how long he was away. He died of epilepsy. I was there.'

A further line of defence, which Burke endeavoured to exploit, was that of provocation. Several Maasai were called to give evidence of their relationship with cattle hand-reared from birth. Under cross-examination

Ranan explained how 'The Accused had nursed the bullock after its mother had died and was particularly attached to it for that reason. The Accused had sold other bullocks from time to time, but would not part with this one.' Others gave of their own experiences, tribal policeman Tigane explaining how he had 'nursed my own sick calf that lost its mother until it recovered. In such a case where you had reared the calf yourself you would look on it as your God. It is dearer to you than all the others.' Karambu's cousin, Merepari, spoke similarly that 'if I nurse a sick calf back to life I dearly love that calf. It is as dearly loved as a child nursed back to life.'

The elder, Katina, went a step further in putting the whole disastrous event in its broader context. 'The Maasai are very attached to their cattle. They don't like at all the requisitions of cattle. They knew the requisition was a government order. If a calf has lost its mother and is sick and the owner nurses it back to health he is even more attached to it, for it is fed like a human being.'

The Crown closed its evidence, with a final statement from its fifteenth witness, Waweru ole Sunyandat, described as a tribal retainer. 'Accused was taken up to where Major Grant was lying on the ground. When I was about to handcuff him he stretched his arms forward. I heard Accused say looking at Major Grant, "Is he dead?" I said "Yes".'

As soon as the Crown rested its case, Burke made a submission to the judge, the gist of which was that he had been briefed to defend the Accused at very short notice and that during the evidence the question of epilepsy had been raised on several occasions. He would therefore like to have his client put under specialist observation following which the expert observer might be able to give evidence material to the defence. Stacey raised no objection despite describing his learned friend's application as 'rather embarrassing', and the judge responded that he felt 'bound to accede to the application' and accordingly granted it.

So on 11 September, Karambu was remanded in the custody of a psychiatric expert for ten days in Nairobi Prison, the case to be resumed in Narok two weeks later. Most of those ten days he spent in Mathari Mental Hospital under the observation of its resident physician, Dr J. C. D. Carothers.

***

When the court reassembled on Wednesday, 25 September, the case for the defence began with the Accused giving evidence on his own affirmation, reiterating how he had 'given a number of oxen to the government during the war for a price. I had so disposed of 25. I had no other bullock than this pet bullock left. I asked Major Grant to let me have back the bullock. I intended to keep it in my stock. I would have gone and searched for another bull for Major Grant from my brothers who had other bullocks.' He then went on: 'I have had one epileptic fit. When I was a youth once and again when I was in Nairobi recently I also fell.'

The defence then called the first of only two substantive witnesses, Ng'abwal ole Mbatian, an uncle of Karambu who testified to a history of epilepsy in the family. Acknowledging that Karambu's father was so affected he then continued. 'I have not been affected. Sendeu died from epilepsy. Ranan has not been affected. Letoile has been affected. He lies if he says he has not been affected. Accused has once been affected … I saw Sendeu when he died. He died on account of a fit which he had for ten days.'

Thereafter the defence's second witness, Dr Carothers, took the stand, and it was probably no surprise to Burke that the doctor's evidence was insufficient to support a plea of insanity, despite Karambu possibly having had a fit while in Mathari. 'I have had Accused under my observation from 13 to 22 September. I think it quite possible that he suffers from occasional epileptic fits', but, he went on…

I came to the conclusion that the crime, the subject of this case, could not be called an epileptic crime… in all these facts there is nothing to suggest that the crime occurred due to an epileptic furor or to epilepsy. There is no evidence in the above cited facts that the Accused was suffering from insanity at the time of the crime … I will go a little further. There is no evidence of mental confusion at the time of the act, no evidence of ill-directed violence towards the victim - the violence in this case was well directed - and no evidence of loss of memory afterwards.

This seemed to damn any chance of insanity as a successful defence, and in his twenty minutes of closing remarks, summarized in ten lines in the written proceedings, Burke was left to focus on the possibility that Grant had provoked Karambu into murdering him by refusing to return Lemelelu. Reminding the court of the particular love of the Maasai for their stock, he suggested that the removal of Karambu's cherished animal might in itself be sufficient to amount to provocation.

When Stacey's turn came, he only needed ten minutes to emphasize Karambu's sanity. He explained how normal the Accused's behaviour had been in asking for the return of his bullock, how an interval of fifteen minutes had elapsed between Grant's refusal to comply with his request and his throwing the spear, and how he then collected up the spear, and after being caught by his brothers, spoke perfectly normally to them. Nowhere was there any evidence of epilepsy (which therefore implied none of insanity), and nor of provocation.

Summing up to the assessors, much as he would have done to a jury, the learned judge reviewed the defence's arguments against the charge of murder. That the Accused had thrown the spear which killed Grant was not in doubt, but could he have been provoked into doing so? No. There was 'no evidence of any provocation given by Major Grant' and 'there is no evidence at all of any wrongful act or insult on the part of Major Grant, and before an accused person can successfully put forward a case of legal provocation it has to be shown…that a wrongful act or insult had been committed by the person killed'.

In dealing with the question of provocation, the judge clearly needed to stress the importance of the time lapse between Grant's refusal to return or exchange the bullock and Karambu throwing the spear. 'There was no question of a forthwith retaliation' he told the assessors and 'some little time did elapse' between the two events.

Whether Major Grant spoke in Swahili or whether the Accused spoke Maasai, there can be no doubt that they were at one in understanding each other; one was asking for the return of his pet ox which he had nursed back to health and strength and the DC said '*hapana*'. However often the request may have been repeated it met with the answer '*hapana*'. Well the evidence as to time - it is always so in cases of this kind - can never be certain. You have already been referred to it by one of the native witnesses who said 'it was a little long time - about as long as I have been in the witness box'. That was the evidence of Letoile, the Accused's brother, when he said it was as long as he had been in the witness box, but it is very difficult to know whether he really appreciated how long he had been in the witness box; but perhaps there is more reliable evidence in the evidence given by Mr Munro. Mr Munro fixes the intervening time, i.e. the time between the valuing and buying of the black ox and the incident, which is the death of Major Grant, as twenty minutes.

Thus dismissing any defence of provocation, the judge then turned to the possibility of Karambu's insanity. Did such evidence as there was of epilepsy, amount to insanity? Sheridan set out the law for the assessors:

> Legal insanity is something very precise and is defined, and a person basing his defence on legal insanity must prove in the first place that he was suffering from a disease of the mind at the time he committed the act, and if he succeeds in proving that, he must then prove either that he did not know the nature of his act - the meaning of that is illustrated in this way that he does not know, for instance, whether he is plunging his spear into a human being or a pig - or that he did not know that the act he was committing was wrong.

The judge continued, explaining how the onus was on the accused person to discharge the presumption of legal sanity. 'Is there any evidence that he has done that?' he asked rhetorically, before answering his own question by reminding the assessors that Dr Carothers had not found the Accused insane. Indeed, he had considered Grant's refusal to return the animal to Karambu as actually providing 'a rational motive' for the killing of the District Commissioner.

With the duty of the assessors being in some way to bridge the divide between the customs and practices of their society and the application of justice under the English legal system, their role was only an advisory one. None of Ole Sengali, Ndelamere or Ole Sawani seemed in any doubt as to Karambu's guilt. Indeed, the second of them to respond to the judge went further than simply rejecting Karambu's defence, also adding his own suggestions as to how the Accused should have handled Grant's refusal to return his bullock:

> We have heard all the evidence. Accused's family suffer from epilepsy and that Accused was attacked once. I don't think the Accused was suffering from epilepsy when he followed the ox. If he was suffering from madness when going to the cattle crush he would have been discovered by others. It is true that he did not expose to anyone he was going to do any such thing at the crush. [He] was not discovered by anyone to be annoyed. If he was discovered to be annoyed he would have been taken far away and not allowed to kill the *bwana*. We find he loved the bullock as he loved it. Another difficulty was he didn't present his case about the return of the ox to the chiefs or elders who would have made an effort to

get it back. He did not converse with *bwana* for long. I want government to realize this is a crime committed by one man.

None of the assessors found any evidence of insanity or of provocation, so Sheridan's verdict was a foregone conclusion. Referring to English case law in support of his decisions, he stressed how, if epilepsy was to sustain the defence of insanity, it must be proved to have existed at the time of the commission of the crime, and this it had not been. So far as provocation was concerned, the point was not whether Karambu was easily provoked, or a particularly volatile character, but rather whether a normal, reasonable man would have been provoked into doing what Karambu did, and the answer was also 'no'.

'The death sentence was then passed' reads the final line of the *East African Standard*'s report, although it does not describe whether the judge donned a black cap to pronounce his words of condemnation:

> The sentence of the Court is, 'Karambu ole Sendeu, you are sentenced to be hanged by the neck until you are dead. May the Lord have mercy on your soul. You have, as I am bound to inform you, thirty days within which to appeal.'

Karambu's horizons had stretched up to the highest tree-covered ridges of the Loita Hills or far across the game-covered plains every day of his life until the day he threw the spear - 16 August 1946. If he could have imagined the realities of life imprisonment in Nairobi's gaol, no doubt he would have restrained his advocate from appealing against the judge's decision. If communication between client and advocate had been easier, then perhaps Burke would have found a way into Karambu's thoughts. As it was, he felt a responsibility to do everything in his power at least to have the death sentence commuted. So appeal Burke did, surely more in hope than expectation of success, to His Majesty's Court of Appeal for Eastern Africa sitting in Dar es Salaam in Tanganyika.

A tribunal of three judges heard the case, and on 15 November 1946, issued a two-paragraph judgment, which ended any chance of the law substituting a gaol sentence for the loss of the prisoner's life. It is damning in its clarity:

> This appeal raises no question of any difficulty whatever either as to the facts or the law. As to the facts it was proved - and indeed admitted - that the appellant threw his spear at Major Grant with such accurate aim and such violence that the spear passed

right through the body of Major Grant and caused his death.

The only defences suggested were prov-ocation sufficient in law to reduce the of-fence to manslaughter and insanity at the time of the killing. These two defences were carefully considered by the learned Chief Justice who came to the conclusion that neither of these defences could be main-tained on the evidence. In our view that was a correct conclusion. Indeed no other conclusion was possible. We therefore find that there is no substance in the appeal and it is dismissed.

Stark government forms and the briefest of memoranda evidence the remainder of Karambu's life. Prison Form No. 38 is the petition form on which the petitioner appeals to the Governor, Sir Philip Mitchell, for mercy, his left thumb print impressed on a typed supporting letter in which he agreed 'I committed the offence, but I was quite out of my mind when I threw the spear. It was not my intention to commit murder. I did so in a fit of temper.' The petition is followed three weeks later by Prison Form No. 42, headed in bold capital letters 'Medical Report upon Prisoner Remanded on a Capital Charge'. It is this which reveals Karambu's mother to be still alive, and that he is childless and single, but otherwise it gives no help to anyone entrusted with the task of reviewing the case. Signed by Dr Carothers, opposite each of the listed habits of alcohol, bhang, tobacco and miraa is typed 'denied' and in the space for 'recommendations' the doctor blandly states that 'there are no medical recommendations'.

Karambu then became minute 17/47 on the agenda of the discussions of the Executive Council of the Colony and Protectorate of Kenya in the first week of 1947. According to the note of these discussions, 'The Governor's Deputy in Council decided that in this case the law should take its course.' So was dismissed the plea for mercy.

Before Karambu's life was ended, there occurred a bizarre exchange of internal administrative correspondence as to the propriety of allowing family members to witness his death. According to Bailward, acting as Officer in Charge Maasai, this was 'the only certain way I know of convincing the Maasai generally that the sentence has been carried into effect'. In response to this he was informed peremptorily by one of his fellow administrators of the existence of 'rulings about this which should have been looked up before this proposal was submitted'. Then Bailward was told only that 'it would be in order for the relatives of the condemned man to view the corpse after execution'.

Whether they did is not recorded, although it seems unlikely, and the final entry in the file of Karambu's life is simply headed 'Report of Execution'. It shows that the young Maasai man had his last look at the bright Kenyan sky on the morning of 28 January 1947, before the trap door opened below his feet and he was 'hanged by the neck until dead'.

**

There were to be several twists in the tale of this black bullock, Lemelelu.

Bailward, as the senior administrator in the Maasai Reserve, and Grant's immediate superior, heard of the District Commissioner's death by way of a phone call put through to him at the Karen Store. This was some seven miles out of town and half way back to his Ngong home and headquarters. Most likely he had stopped there to buy provisions, or was perhaps flagged down on the road to take the urgent message. He immediately headed back to Nairobi for discussions with the Chief Secretary, the Chief Native Commissioner and the magistrate, Wainwright. At 8.45 p.m. he returned to Ngong, leaving home by lorry two hours later, and reaching Narok at 5.00 a.m. the following morning to begin his inquiries.

The Administration's immediate concern after arresting Karambu was that the whole incident would

spark massive unrest amongst a community already
known for its intolerance, not only of the cattle quota
purchase scheme, but also of the colonial government
in general. The Administration certainly took comfort
from the capture of Karambu by his own brothers, but it
would have been with some trepidation that Bailward,
Assistant Inspector of Police Mills, and 27 men left
Narok for the Loita Hills later on Saturday.

Arriving in Morijo Bailward found that most of
the Maasai appeared as shocked by Grant's murder as
were the DC's fellow Europeans, although Karambu's
troublesome Engedongi relatives had made themselves
very scarce. Bailward kept a detailed, and carefully typed
diary in which he recorded the tenor of his address to a
meeting of about 30 Loita elders, headed by Chief ole
Parkishwaa, who was there awaiting his arrival in the
Loita Hills:

> They seemed to be inclined to adopt
> the attitude that they were not to blame
> for the occurrence. I reminded them of
> the events that led to it - i.e. Major Grant
> finding no cattle brought in on the 15th
> and that no efforts were being made to
> bring in any stock, took the only course
> open to him and proceeded to direct req-
> uisitioning of cattle from the *bomas* of the

influential and prosperous Engedongi. Subsequently, when these cattle were in the course of sale, together with others requisitioned from the school *boma* (and still no cattle voluntarily brought in) Major Grant became the victim of a cowardly and vindictive attack from behind, which deprived the Maasai of a loyal friend and the service of a gallant and honourable officer. This had happened in their country, primarily owing to their failure to bring in their stock...

Moreover, in the eyes of the world, which knew nothing of the Loita or the Engedongi, a good and gallant friend had been killed by the Maasai and their name, not too popular at the present time, would suffer still further.

Having set his tone, Bailward then ordered that the Maasai immediately make good the balance of the quota, which Grant and Munro had started to fill with requisitioned cattle. He also ordered that they cooperate fully with police inquiries. To both of these orders they agreed, and were in deed as good as their word. Nonetheless, Bailward made sure to stress that this would not be the end of the matter, and nor was it.

By notice in the Kenya Gazette of 1 October 1946 Bailward appointed Ng'abwal ole Mbatian, Karambu's uncle and witness for his defence, as 'official headman' of the Engedongi Area, presumably in an effort to fit a more amenable character into the section's hierarchy. About the same time, in order to try and further limit the pernicious influence of the Engedongi, Bailward placed its members in effective quarantine.

Forced to justify these actions as a result of complaints of unreasonable restraint from certain Maasai, through their Nairobi lawyers, Messrs Shapley, Schwarze & Barret, he wrote to the Chief Secretary on 12 November 1946. First, he gave some background, describing the Engedongi as 'a very powerful and malign influence in that its members are traditional witch doctors for the Maasai tribe and, by means of the charms that they sell to the young men, are indirectly responsible for much of the stock theft and on occasions for murder that is committed by Maasai *moran*'. Thereafter, Bailward explained how, in response to this influence, which the arrest of Karambu may well have strengthened, he had 'issued orders which have been promulgated through their headman that members of the Engedongi section should not leave their areas without permission from the District Commissioner...and through the headmen of all sections that Maasai of *moran* age were forbidden to visit the Engedongi *laibons*'. A police detachment of eight men, with its own wireless set, was stationed in the area to enforce the orders.

Bailward was also responsible for raising the question of compensation with the Maasai, a subject which was to gather its own momentum. After discussions with the Chief Secretary and others, it was felt that, since Grant would never have been murdered if the full quota of cattle had been voluntarily offered up for sale, the Maasai should make further recompense. It was long established Maasai custom to expiate murders by payment of cattle, and Bailward records in his diary how he suggested that '500 head of good cattle of a value of not less than £2,000 would seem reasonable compensation in this ... I went so far as to say that government would be prepared to enforce such a payment but wished to give them the opportunity first of saying whether they would pay this amount of compensation'. This they immediately agreed to do 'without withdrawing for consultation'.

The Administration suspected that the alacrity with which the Maasai accepted the suggestion indicated they had, in fact, expected a much more severe penalty. It was no surprise, therefore, when the 500 cattle were quickly offered up - nor perhaps that the quality was such as only to realize £1,971, just short of the agreed minimum of £2,000.

Meanwhile, Pauline, who had left Kenya for Scotland two months after her husband's death, had invested the compensation payment with its own mystique, convinced that it was a spontaneous gesture by the Maasai community for the benefit of her three children. While some within the Administration were concerned that the compensation should not be construed by the outside world as a voluntary act of contrition, no one in authority was inclined to disabuse her.

The sum of £1,971, which would otherwise have been paid to the Maasai for their cattle, was therefore settled on the trustees of a Trust dated 20 February 1947. One of its introductory recitals reads, 'And whereas certain members of the Maasai tribe of Kenya aforesaid have donated... the sum of one thousand nine hundred and seventy one pounds to be applied towards the advancement and education of the children [of Grant]'. Two of the three trustees were ex officio - J. F. G. Troughton, Financial Secretary of the government, and P. W. Harris, Acting Chief Native Commissioner - and the third, Dr Gerald V. W. Anderson, a close friend of Grant and his wife and the person largely responsible for rekindling their spiritual and religious inclinations.

7

AFTERWORD

These are the circumstances of the case as gleaned primarily from witness statements in the Administration's files in the Kenya National Archives. The file on Karambu's murder trial covers not only the preliminary inquiry and the trial itself, but also the appeal to the Court of Appeal and petition for clemency to the Governor of the Colony and Protectorate of Kenya. Valuable background information is also contained in the Handing Over Reports prepared by outgoing District Commissioners for their successors, as well as in each DC's Annual Report on the state of Narok District.

None of the details of this story is imagined, and if there are mistakes, they are probably a consequence of inaccurate deductions from the available evidence. For example, the plan of the crime scene, prepared by the Narok police inspector I. V. B. Mills, shows both blood and a cigar butt on the ground where Grant's body ended up; I therefore presume he was smoking when he was speared. The details of the clothes he was wearing at the time his body was examined are set out in the post-mortem report, so it seems reasonable to assume he dressed in them in the early morning.

Grant's life is written about in some detail in his daughter, Anne Goldsmith's family biography *Gentle Warrior*, even to the extent of his drinking a glass of sherry with Pauline before their final farewell and her departure for Nairobi. Reconstructing Karambu's life is much more difficult and a question of overlaying the strict Maasai age system on such details of his life as emerged from the trial, and placing the whole in the physical context of Morijo. This does indeed entail some sweeping assumptions.

The witness statements are all written in English, almost faultlessly typed out on numbered pages. Most Maasai witnesses gave verbal evidence in their own language, which was then translated into Swahili, and thence into English, so direct speech attributed to them is third hand. This process of judicial Chinese whispers was a laborious one, which inevitably blunted the edge of a lot of their evidence. In some places it may even have altered the meaning, notwithstanding that most of the British administrators, and this would include court personnel, spoke very good Swahili. It may also give particular veracity to those witnesses who gave their evidence directly in English, particularly the cattle buyer, William Munro, who was with Grant right up to the moment of his death.

Court stenographers were usually painstakingly accurate in their reporting, although they tended to pare down some of the witness statements, and also often omitted the question that produced a reported reply. While both the *East African Standard* and the court proceedings have Munro saying how 'in the second *manyatta*, there were various old men and several of them objected to our taking all the cattle', only the *Standard* reports Stacey asking, 'When you say the cattle were taken by force did anybody remonstrate?' The court and the newspaper sometimes represented the same direct speech slightly differently, although seldom to the extent of missing the point. The *Standard* reported Munro as saying, somewhat sensationally, 'During these exciting moments, I did not see Major Grant; I was following the chase', as against the court's more sombre reporting: 'I did not see Major Grant then, I had climbed up the rails to see how the chase was getting on'.

Many of the witnesses provided statements both at the preliminary inquiry, held to determine if there was sufficient evidence to support a prosecution, and also at Karambu's trial, which followed it. There is generally a marked consistency between the evidence given at the two sets of proceedings, although occasionally either memories were confused or speech misreported. Karambu's brother, Letoile, who had been at the *ol pul* with him, described at the preliminary inquiry how he 'explained to the Accused that his bullock, mentioning it by name, Lemelelu, had been taken' and that 'Accused made no comment but said we had better go and get our money'. Yet at the trial, Letoile recalled that on meeting Karambu, 'I told Accused that the bullocks had been taken away. I did not mention his bullock Lemelelu. I said all the oxen had been taken.'

At the root of the tragedy lay a colonizer's scheme for the compulsory acquisition of cattle from members of a tribe which not only set unmatched store by its independence but also imbued its cattle with a near-spiritual significance. The pastoral Maasai way of life had always been lived uneasily beneath the spreading umbrella of central government interference, as it still is today. In 1946 it was the British colonial administration that seemed determined to destroy their traditional systems of stock management - and principally for the benefit of Britain. Each Maasai was already a member of the tribe, as well as of a section or clan of that tribe, and the idea of also existing as part of a nation state was completely alien. This applied not least to the Maasai of the Loita Hills, whose annual grazing cycles took many of them over the unmarked borders between the separate political entities of the Colony and Protectorate of Kenya and Tanganyika Territory.

For the previous six years, the Maasai had been asked to find cattle to feed people living far beyond the borders of their known world, whose needs were driven by the economic consequences of a war which had been none of their concern. To add considerable insult to this injury, the same government to call for the Maasai's cattle was forbidding them from raiding their neighbours in an attempt to seize enough animals to satisfy the very quotas imposed upon them. This government would also not hesitate to introduce quarantine regulations, which not only thwarted the traditional migrations in search of better grazing, but by confining cattle in enclosed areas, actually contributed to the very overstocking of which it complained.

Few of those responsible for implementing the livestock purchase scheme would have argued, at least in August 1946, for its total abandonment. When he gave evidence at Karambu's trial Bailward cast no doubts on the way the scheme as a whole had been managed, and even went so far as to praise the Maasai for their cooperation. However, Grant's murder focused the spotlight on its *modus operandi*, particularly in the Maasai Reserve, and must have given those involved, at the very least, some cause for reflection. When handing over to R. A. Wilkinson in 1946, following his temporary stewardship of Narok after the District Commissioner's death, Bailward wrote, 'So far as meat stock is concerned, the Maasai of this end [Narok District] have been pretty mercilessly flogged and you cannot get blood out of a stone...' And at the end of the year, by the time he came to relinquish his post as Officer-in-Charge of the whole Maasai Reserve, Bailward admitted that 'the Maasai had been overbought and are sick to death of Control buying'.

While in no way absolving the Engedongi section of their failure to bring in cattle voluntarily, was Bailward in fact intimating that by the time of Grant's killing, too much was being asked of the Maasai in terms of supplying cattle? In his three-month 1946 tenure as Narok DC, Wilkinson seems to have come to a similar conclusion. In the Annual Report of Narok District for that year he wrote that, over the year as a whole...

> The Maasai Elders were not uncooperative in...the production of beef for the Livestock Control. For the first six months of the year collection was made on the basis of 1,800 head every two months (or 2,000 a month for all Maasai). In Narok,

the numbers of beasts brought forward were considerably less than the quota, and the fourth sale of the year was devoted to recovering arrears. Eventually it was decided that two more reduced quotas of 1,350 should be collected, making a total of 8,100 head for the year. By the end of the year 7,212 cattle had been collected...these cattle were brought in without much difficulty (except for the unfortunate occasion when Major Grant was killed) and represented a considerable sacrifice by the Maasai; an inspection of the herds makes it clear that there are extremely few good bullocks left.

'*A considerable sacrifice by the Maasai; an inspection of the herds makes it clear that there are extremely few good bullocks left*'. During his cross-examination, Karambu had explained how, 'Other than this bull, I have ten cows left. The 25 I sold to government have been over a period during the war. I have sent five head of cows to government during last eight or nine months.' When his time came to give evidence, the elder, Katina ole Legei, described how he 'leant to try and cut off the bell that was round the neck of my animal'. Bells would have adorned the necks of the most favoured and reliable animals, and usually the last to be submitted for any sale. If these details are correct and Karambu's figures show a snapshot of the cattle purchase scheme in action, it begins to look as if the regulations by which the scheme was administered had failed to keep pace with the reality of the situation in the field. There had been a desperate need for beef during the war but by 1946, had the demand lost track of the providers' ability to supply? To paraphrase Winston Churchill, had too much been asked of too few by too many?

Wilkinson spent over five years as District Commissioner for Narok, so in his 1951 Handing Over Report he was able to comment with the benefit of considerable hindsight on the situation he inherited in 1946:

> There is no doubt that by the end of the war, male stock had been over-bought in Narok District, and the sales had become very unpopular. One of the most unpopular features was the fact that Livestock Control had a monopoly of buying, and it became apparent that the Maasai would not be likely to bring forward cattle for sale with any willingness until they could see other buyers...in the ring.

From the British perspective, Kenya needed feeding, as did the Allied troops during the war, and the Maasai had the wherewithal to make a major contribution to food supplies - something they would only do if forced. On top of this, for any one of a variety or reasons outlined earlier, their pastures tended to be so drastically overstocked as to risk becoming permanently degraded.

The compulsory purchase scheme, albeit one in which the government was the only buyer, realized the twin objectives of providing regular meat supplies and attaining a more optimal stocking density - at least from the government's perspective. Yet after Grant's death, we start to see repeated references to the programme as basically overplayed and exhausted. So was Grant actually put into the totally invidious position of being expected to help manage a scheme that had already been flogged to near-death?

Nevertheless, Grant had a job to do in providing cattle for the Livestock Control, and his 'was not to reason why'. He was new to the district, briefed only by a Handing Over Report from his predecessor, although after his short posting to Kajiado five years earlier, not entirely new to the ways of the Maasai. Given the prevailing law of the time, albeit that of the British administration, it was the Engedongi section's culture of passive resistance, manifesting itself in a failure to provide their cattle quota, which set the whole dreadful chain of events in motion.

As no cattle were being voluntarily offered for sale, Grant's terms of reference as the local District Commissioner left him no option but to use his powers to requisition. With Karambu tragically away from his manyatta, Ranan could at least have made representations on behalf of his brother, and didn't. Had he done so, Grant and Munro would surely have accepted a substitute animal, just as they had done an hour earlier in the manyatta which provided the first batch of cattle. Even at Morijo, Grant had allowed an elder to remove one of the requisitioned animals. Yet neither Karambu nor his brother had made any effort to keep Lemelelu out of the sale until the very last minute.

Down at the collecting pen, Grant's *hapana* sealed his fate as effectively as Chief Justice Sheridan's verdict would seal that of his killer. Grant's character is perhaps encapsulated in the title of the book about him - *Gentle Warrior*. Even accepting that a family biography is likely to promote the positive side of its subject's character, whether in title or in text, his bravery was unquestionable, earning him an MC and Bar during the last months of the First World War. Beyond doubt too was the kindness and consideration of others which was nourished by his deep attachment to Christianity. Given the extraordinarily trying and early start to the day occasioned by the need to requisition cattle, Grant's reaction to Karambu's request was surely understandable. However bravery is often enabled by impetuosity, which in many circumstances manifests itself as impatience. Had Friday 16 August 1946 been one of the days when his kindness triumphed over his impatience Grant would most likely have gone that one step further and tried to hear out Karambu.

The file, which otherwise covers the Administration's response to Grant's death, ends with a peculiar letter from a Marjorie P. J. Bennet, writing from Kitale on 16 October 1946, no doubt included there for want of any more suitable resting place:

> I am interested in the case of the native who stabbed Major Grant. Tho' I thoroughly realize that the decision to take his bullock may have been made thro' strain and tiredness and Major Grant was tired of arguing, and while I am very sorry for Mrs Grant and her children, I do still feel sorry for the native. I do not know the procedure in these cases, but would be very grateful if you could find time to let me know if there was any drug or hypnotic treatment which he could have to enable him to go on thinking he had his bullock with him and that tho' he may have to pay the penalty for

his action that people still do understand. Unfortunately I have not much money at the moment but I would be grateful if you could let me know if such treatment were possible, and if so, how much it would cost.

The request is unusual, to say the least, particularly in the colonial context of 1946, and one of the internal memos following it describes the writer as a 'crank'. Still, the letter certainly identifies what must have been at least one of the prevailing opinions among the settler community - that Grant's behaviour on the fateful day was influenced by 'strain and tiredness'.

Grant is sure to have spoken excellent Swahili, but Karambu could only remonstrate with him in Maa. Had communication been more direct, had Grant been able to understand such reasoned representations as Karambu may have presented, he might have been persuaded of Karambu's attachment to Lemelelu, and the spear would never have been thrown. Nor perhaps might it have been if Grant had a more intimate understanding of the culture of the Maasai and their relationship with their cattle than he had been able to acquire from his short time in Kajiado and five months in Narok.

No evidence was produced to say that Karambu had himself actively participated in the refusal to supply the Engedongi's Friday cattle quota – whether or not he did would anyway not have affected his culpability. On the contrary, under cross-examination he was certainly shown to have cooperated fully with the Administration to the extent of providing cattle during earlier quota requests.

During the court case, the Loita elder, Katina, contended that he and his kinsmen 'had no information about sending cattle in' for sale at Morijo that Friday. Ranan also alleged that 'we had received no previous information'. If there was truth in these assertions, it would explain the apparent lack of concern at what might be happening at home, which Karambu evinced in disappearing off to a meat camp three days earlier, and not returning until the day of the sale. Or otherwise, might the Administration have communicated its instructions to produce animals for sale to the senior Engedongi elders, who had decided among themselves not to do so, without informing other members of the clan of their decision?

During the preliminary inquiry Ranan had given evidence that he 'saw Major Grant laugh at the young man, Accused, and then turn back to the pen, lean on the rails and continue to watch the sales and read out the price of each animal'. Had Grant laughed at Karambu, that might well have constituted provocation sufficient to support such a defence in the actual trial. Yet Burke never raised the question of laughter in the trial itself and no one, least of all the Chief Justice, found anything provocative in Grant's behaviour. 'I find the Accused killed Major Grant who at the time had committed no wrongful act or insult, according to the evidence … No case of legal provocation is revealed in the evidence…'

One possible influence on Karambu's behaviour, to which no reference was ever made in the trial, was his drinking the soup which most likely supplemented the meat-only regime in the *ol pul* camp. Such soup was usually first prepared in two separate vessels, one containing herbs and the other meat. The two would then be stirred up together and decanted into a single cow-horn cup for drinking. The concoction was foremost an aid to the digestion of consecutive meals of heavy protein, but the mixture varied, depending on who was taking it and the nature of the occasion.

The barks of *Acacia nilotica (olkiloriti)* and *Acacia mellifera (oiti)* both aid digestion, as do the roots of the liana, *Rhamnus prenoides (olkonyil)*. Groups of young men would be just as likely to add stimulants to the mix. The strength of these additives would vary depending upon the activities for which the men were preparing. If *moran* were gathered together in readiness for a lion hunt or cattle raid, this might call for a powerful stimulant such as provided by boiling the roots of *Pappea capensis (oltimigomi)*. In the forested areas grew the climber *Toddalia asiatica* with a legion of uses, including the suppression of pain. The potency of any preparation could be varied by adding more or less of a particular ingredient.

While Karambu may not have been a warrior any longer, he had just recently graduated to junior elder and many of his *moran* manners will have endured through into this new stage of life. He had only left the *ol pul* that morning. If some of the soup had been mixed in such a way as to blur judgement or engender feelings of invulnerability or irresponsibility, those effects might easily have lingered in his system until he arrived at the collecting pens. If, on top of his anger and distress, he still felt buoyed by an aura of invincibility, which effectively disconnected the act of killing the District Commissioner from the consequences of doing so, then surely the spear became that much easier to throw.

Karambu does not seem to have died a martyr to some anti-colonial cause, with the Maasai as a whole determined to avenge his execution. Rather, most Maasai became more inclined to shun the Engedongi section, for fear of guilt by association, than to foment their own anti-Administration responses. After all, it was his brothers who actually arrested him, Ranan describing how, when he caught up with Karambu, he had questioned him as to why he had done 'such a big thing as this', to which Karambu had replied that 'he was caught by madness'. So Ranan took him back to the collecting pens and handed him over to a tribal policeman saying 'take him and shoot him'.

One of the assessors, in response to the judge's summing up, gave a surprising sense of his community's concern for the consequences of Karambu's actions when commenting that 'We have heard about this youth and what he has done'. He then continued. 'We Maasai did not sit and consult to do such a big thing as this. Since he committed this thing we thought best to hand him to the government as we don't want to die for one man's act.'

Whatever the reactions of the Administration, there is no denying that the same colonial government to impose the compulsory purchase of cattle on the Maasai, also imposed a penal code far removed from that under which Karambu and his kinsfolk lived and died. Had Karambu suffered for his crimes under his own tribal law, his penalty was likely to have been very different. In a society where life was precarious enough already, there seemed no sense in adding to the death toll through punishment, and the emphasis was more on restorative than retributive justice. Rather than punish offenders, much better to have them make some form of recompense. While it was not unknown for the brothers of a murdered man to avenge their loss with the death of the killer, more likely was punishment through the payment of cattle. In his classic monograph *The Masai* Moritz Merker described how...

> In some districts, no difference is made between premeditated murder and unintentional killing, as for example, in Loita, where also blood-revenge is very seldom practised. In this district the murderer loses all of his possessions as punishment for the murder or manslaughter of a man; his cattle, wives and children all pass to the heir of his victim.

With both the British and Maasai so resolutely convinced of the superiority of their own respective ways of life, was it not almost inevitable that a tragedy of this nature would happen somewhere, some day? And is it not astonishing, and perhaps a credit to both, that their cultures did not clash so tragically more often? Perversely, many British administrators found themselves respecting the pride, even arrogance, of many of their Maasai 'subjects' despite this often translating into an overt contempt for the colonizers. Throughout British Empire history, its officers have seldom hidden a respect for 'the noble savage' who acted through strength rather than guile, whose word was his bond. With their impressive physique and warlike demeanour the Maasai certainly fitted this ideal.

The Maasai were renowned for their scorn of manual or menial work. For them their work was their life - caring for livestock. They nurtured a disdain for outsiders and a conviction that whatever happened beyond the borders of Maasailand need be none of their concern unless they were going there on cattle raids. The colonial imposition of a central government, uniting disparate ethnic groups into a single nation state, was complete anathema to them.

By 1951, the Administration's ambivalence to the influence of the *laibons* had changed little. When Wilkinson was handing over to J. Pinney, he noted how the *laibons* still 'carry out a certain amount of legitimate functions such as administering medicines and officiating at certain tribal ceremonies'. Then he went on to add that '...they also provide charms for the *moran* to ensure the success of stock raiding forays, and have other fairly harmful functions'.

Other things did change for the better, at least from the Maasai perspective. In the same report Wilkinson wrote how...

> Arrangements were accordingly made with the rather reluctant consent of the Meat Marketing Board [which took over from Livestock Control] for selected Kikuyu butchers from Kiambu and Somali butchers resident in Maasai to attend the Narok and Naroosura sales, and for butchers from Kisii township to attend the Kilgoris sales. This proved a great success from the Maasai point of view, and has resulted in respectable numbers of cattle being brought forward for the sales. At Narok and Naroosura the Somalis and Kikuyu normally outbid the Meat Marketing Board...and buy all that is offered in the early stages of the sale...I have noticed a definite change in the attitude of the Maasai to these cattle sales since competitive buying and good prices prevailed.

Today, there are as many versions of this story as there are Maasai - and Europeans - prepared to relate it. Karambu is remembered by most of those old enough to have heard the tale from anyone alive at the time, if not as a hero, then at least as a very brave man. He is also generally reckoned to have actually produced several other cattle and offered on the spot to exchange these for Lemelelu, but to no avail.

The isolation imposed upon the Engedongi by Bailward, which both prevented members of the section from leaving their home area, and outsiders from visiting the *laibons*, gets a life of its own; through successive tellings, this has been embellished to include most of the Loita Maasai in this effective 'quarantine'.

What may seem remarkable now, in the light of the ease of transport and communications, is that most Maasai in the Loita Hills still seem to have no idea of Karambu's eventual fate. That he was taken off to Narok is well recognized, but what happened thereafter is not, and certainly once he was removed to Nairobi his fellows appear to have lost all touch with him. Having no wife or children, and his relatives perhaps being fearful of the consequences of claiming kinship, those close to him seem simply to have let the trail go cold. Yet, set against the background of 1946, when vehicles seldom entered the Loita Hills, most of its residents had not even visited Narok, and few Maasai were educated enough to read any newspapers that did reach Morijo, this is perhaps not actually surprising at all.

The European attitude to the whole affair has doubtless changed with the passing of time. When Grant was killed, the incident horrified both the settler community and the Administration. Such horror would have been tempered by a degree of relief that, as Bailward had written when handing over to Wilkinson, and most others believed, 'it was an individual crime committed for no sufficient cause by a vindictive young man of the Engedongi section'.

Against the backdrop of colonial Kenya, the imposition of the death penalty on Karambu was inevitable. Killing any executive officer was a heinous crime, striking at the very foundations of the colony's administration. True, the government seems to have ensured that Karambu was provided with the best available legal representation. His counsel, Burke, offered the defence of provocation, and, perhaps pushing his brief almost too far, also suggested that an epileptic fit may have affected his client's behaviour. This resulted in a two-week adjournment, and on the failure of both those defences, Burke then appealed to the East African Court of Appeal. Yet, perhaps the cultural divide between the Accused and his counsel was simply too great for the one to be able to take real advantage of the services offered by the other.

Some Europeans may have had their reservations over what they saw as Grant's intransigence, especially if they regarded the incident in isolation - as starting and ending at the Morijo cattle collecting pens. To make any sort of rational judgement, either then or now, Grant's actions need to be set against the whole background of the quota system that it was his duty to enforce, and the legal requirement for him to requisition cattle in the event that these were not offered for sale voluntarily.

Perhaps judgement is better reserved for the quota system itself, although this looks a very different undertaking now, than it did against the immediate aftershocks of a World War and of the worldwide food shortages that followed it. And of course, that quota system was only an integral part of the greater colonial administration of Kenya, and this too is only properly judged in the context of its time, rather than by the codes and conduct of today.

ADDENDA

Notes on the text

There may be different ways to spell the same Maa word, often depending on the historical context in which it is used. So, in all the Administration's reports, 'Engedongi' is the spelling of the section of the 'Masai'. Now, 'Maasai' is more usual and Engedongi has become Inkidongi, Enkidongi or Nkidongi. For consistency, I have changed Masai to Maasai wherever it appears but Engedongi remains. The same goes for certain place names which were spelt differently in 1940s reports than they are now, as well as for the names of prominent Maasai. Mbatian and his sons, Lenana and Sendeu, can each be spelt in a variety of ways and my choices may usually be seen as the most colloquial.

I have also allowed other minor changes to quotations so that the end result fits better with the rest of the text. Thus complete accuracy of quotations has been sacrificed for greater editorial consistency throughout.

I generally use the place names that would have prevailed at the time about which I am writing, so Lake Rudolf, Abyssinia and Tanganyika (Turkana, Ethiopia and Tanzania).

I have retained a few Maa or Swahili words in the text. Sometimes they appear as such in quoted passages (*baraza*), or maybe there is no obvious English equivalent (*manyatta*); occasionally words are in such common use in East Africa today as to have become part of everyday English vocabulary (*bwana*). When used, these words are all italicized and a translation is usually provided in brackets the first time the word appears. Most of them are also listed with their meanings on the next page.

Some of the Maa words are grammatically imprecise, but are in the form more commonly used in contemporary English/Swahili. *Moran* would be more properly *ol-murrani* or, in the plural, *il-murran*, and *manyatta* is more correctly replaced by *enkang* in the Maasai context.

askari – guard
baraza – meeting
boma – enclosure or government enclave
bwana – boss, important person
emurata – circumcision
hapana – no
laibon – spiritual leader
manyatta – thorn fenced enclosure for humans and animals
moran – warrior
mzee – old person
ole – child of (in names)
ol pul – meat camp
shuka – cloak

Very Select Bibliography

Allan, Susie and Letilet Ole Yenko, *Letilet's Tales* (Shaba Ltd, UK, 2013)

Borwein, Sophie, *Privatizing Pastures: Land Tenure Reform in Kenya's Maasailand* (Public Policy & Governance Review Volume 4, Issue 2, Winter 2013)

Brown Karen and Gilfoyle Daniel (editors), *Healing the Herds* (Ohio University Press, Athens, Ohio, 2010)

Collins, R. L., *Kenya – The Evolution of Independence* (Arthur H. Stockwell Ltd, Devon, England, 2014)

Goldsmith, Anne (editor), *Gentle Warrior* (MPG Books Ltd, Bodmin, 2001)

Hughes, Lotte, *Moving the Maasai – A Colonial Misadventure* (Palgrave Macmillan, 2006)

Huxley Elspeth, *White Man's Country* (Chatto and Windus, London, 1935)

Jackson Tudor, *The Law of Kenya* (East Africa Literature Bureau, Nairobi, 1970)

Kenya National Archives, particularly Judicial & Legal file 14/1/341, and other files MAA/7/737, AH/13/108, DC/NRK/1/1/4, DC/NRK/2/1/1.

Maundu, P. et al., *Ethnobotany of the Loita Maasai: Towards Community Management of the Forest of the Lost Child - Experiences from the Loita Ethnobotany Project* (People and Plants working paper 8, UNESCO, Paris, 2001)

Merker, M., *Die Masai* (Dietrich Reimer, Berlin, 1904)

Miller, Charles, *The Lunatic Express* (Ballantine Books, 1971)

Mol, Frans, *Maa A dictionary of the Maasai Language and Folklore* (Marketing & Publishing Ltd, Nairobi, Kenya, 1978)

Pavitt, Nigel, *Kenya - A country in the making - 1880-1940*
(W. W. Norton & Co. Ltd, New York & London, 2008)

Spencer, Ian, *Settler Production in Kenya in World War II* (Journal of African History 21, 1980)

Swainson, Nicola, *The Development of Corporate Capitalism in Kenya, 1918-77* (University of California Press, 1980)

Acknowledgements

Thanks are due to many and particularly to...

Susie Allan for helping my researches in the Loita Hills

Archives researcher extraordinaire, Richard Ambani

Tony Archer, Andy Hill, Onesmo Ole MoiYoi and my brother Julian for reading and commenting on various earlier versions

Jack Barrah, Greville Gunson and others who enlightened me about the operation of the cattle quota purchase scheme

Staff of the British Institute of East Africa

John Golds and Michael Aronson for telling me about a DC's life

Emma O'Hea, Bella Grant and other members of the Grant family for supporting the idea of this work, reading an early draft, allowing quotations from *Gentle Warrior* and providing a photograph of Hugh Jan Grootenhuis who introduced me to David ole Ntiyani and whose 'Jan's Camp' near Entesekera in the Loita Hills provided a wonderful base from which to explore them

Clare Hardy for editorial input

John Keen for opening up his formidable memory and sharing some of its contents, as well as for reading one of the later versions of this story

Kenya National Archives for providing access to such a wealth of material, and for having, with help from Syracuse University in Syracuse, New York, catalogued this in such a user-friendly manner

Some wonderfully helpful people in The Ohio State University libraries

David ole Ntiyani for guiding me around the Loita Hills and introducing me to *mzee* Kirisharie ole Koilaand, whom I also thank

Henry ole Saitabau, botanist from the Nairobi herbarium and whose home is in the Loita Hills, for reading and advising

White Man's Country from which I have taken quotations quoted in it

Mary Ann for multifarious help and support